What Others Are Saying On You

"This book is exactly what my husband needs. I know that he would rather ride his motorcycle or cook on the grill than even talk about parenting techniques, but I'm going to give him this book. It is funny and to the point, and it covers the basics of parenting from a regular dad perspective. I know that this book will open a dialogue about our kids that my husband and I don't have now. I am also recommending it to all the women in my classes."

--Kim DeMarchi, M.Ed., C.P.E. (Certified Parent Educator)
Co-Founder, Empowered Parenting
Co-Director, RCB of Los Angeles

"I'm a funny guy...obviously. But raising kids isn't always funny business. With two young children and a doctor for a wife, I don't always feel plugged in to the family dynamic. This book gave me some tools that I can use to get caught up. Plus, it's funny! I read it in two days. I would say it is a must for young dads as well as old-timers like me."

--David Zucker, Writer/Director
Airplane!, The Naked Gun, Scary Movie 3 & 4

I have a very wacky dad. He says random things and he can fart at any time. You would be lucky to have my dad because if you did he would go to all of your sports games, fix all your broken things and make you delicious dinners. I think this book is probably the best book for dads because it has the best advice. I know because my dad always gives me good advice.

--Kate Reilly, Age 9

I think you should read this book. My dad is funny and tells really funny jokes so this book will be funny too. He plays video games and wrestles. He's a really cool dad. Also he likes swimming so there might be some swimming in here.

Luke Reilly age 7

"My daddy" – Brooke Reilly, age 2

You are Going Get Poop On You
An Average Guy's Guide to Being an Extraordinary Dad

by
Joe Reilly

© 2011 Joe Reilly. All rights reserved.
ISBN 978-1-257-82323-9

To Beth and Kate and Luke and Brooke. Without you I am just some guy. But with you I'm Dad.

Table of Contents

FORWARD (For Women Only)..xiii

INTRODUCTION xvii
  Who in the hell is Joe Reilly? xx
  Your Parenting Philosophy xxiii

Chapter 1 – PRE-PREGNANCY - A.K.A. THE LAST TIME YOU'LL BE IN CONTROL OF THIS PROCESS FOR ABOUT A YEAR 1
  Be careful what you wish for..2
  Dadvice 3
  Pick the right wife 3
  Making the baby..4
  My boys can swim 5

Chapter 2 – SO YOU'RE GONNA BE A DAD 8
  The Pregnancy..8
  Months 0-3 9
  Months 4-6 10
  Months 7-9 12
  Dr. Doctor, give me the news..13
  Holy f*****g s**t! The baby is coming! 15
  The hospital 16
  More doctors 17
  The actual birth 18
  A few final thoughts about the pregnancy.............................21

Chapter 3 – THIS MORNING I WAS FRED......NOW I'M..... DADDY? 24
  Boys versus girls..24
  PDSS: Post Delivery Stress Syndrome 26
  Staying in the hospital 26
  The baby tests 27
  Snip snip 28
  Where's the love?..29
  So that's what they're for!..30

Going home 31
The baby at home 31

Chapter 4 – YOU AND YOUR BABY AT 0-6 MONTHS 33
Where are the instructions? 34
Sweet sweet sleep 35
You are going to get poop on you 37
The battle ahead..40
The Magic Bullet..41
Never say never...42
Going back to work 43
This is going to sound stupid, but…..44
Wham bam thank you ma'am..45
Rover and the baby...45

Chapter 5 – RAISING A KID - YOUR BABY AT 6-24 MONTHS 47
Sitting..48
Crawling..48
Pulling Up...49
Walking 50
Cause and effect..50

Chapter 6 – THEY'RE NOT BABIES ANYMORE - YOUR CHILD AT 2-3 YEARS 52
Joestradamous 53
Getting respect..55
But it sounds too hard 57
Do I know enough now? 59
A final word on respect...59

Chapter 7 – YOU'RE A BIG KID NOW, AND SO ARE THEY - YOUR CHILD AT 3-5 YEARS...61
No bossing 62
Seal Team Smith..63
You're in the Army now 65
Sergeant Dad? I don't think so 66
Boys versus girls, part 2..67
Now is that it? 68
Who is this kid? 69
If I'm not special, then what am I?..71

The Lion 71
How to be a Lion 73

Chapter 8 – A FEW OTHER THINGS TO CONSIDER IN THIS AGE RANGE - YOUR CHILD AT 3-5 YEARS (STILL) 76
The emotional bank account 76
Making deposits 77
Core emotions 79
TV 84
The gist of all this 84

CHAPTER 9 – LOOK AT YOU NOW - YOUR CHILD AT 5 YEARS AND BEYOND 86
What happens when they're bigger and stronger than me?...... 86
Making a big deal out of small stuff 88
Answering questions 89
You're a dad again 90
Rebellion 91
Becoming your dad (an adult) 93
Great things about getting older 93

Chapter 10 – YOU'RE NOT ALONE 96

Chapter 11 – THINGS WE'VE SAID 97

Chapter 12 – WE DID DO A FEW THINGS RIGHT 98

CHAPTER 13 – SO WHAT HAVE YOU LEARNED? 99

ADDENDUM 1 – KEY PHRASES TO REMEMBER 103

ADDENDUM 2 – YOUR FINAL TOOLBOX 104

CONTACT ME 105

ABOUT THE AUTHOR 106

DISCLAIMER

The characters and events in this book are real – even though the author sometimes wishes they weren't. Any attempt to replicate the author's experiences with your own children will result in varying degrees of success ranging from joyous, blissful childlike freedom and happiness for you and all your loved ones for eternity to instantaneous fits of animalistic bloodlust and carnal rage set off by the slightest provocation. But you'll probably get the first one.

Possible side effects from reading this book include: feelings of superiority, increased brain size and function leading to possible interspecies communication, and powerful wife-subduing erections. <u>You Are Going To Get Poop On You</u> is not recommended for everyone. Consult you doctor if you feel the urge to talk incessantly about your children or menstruate with every lunar cycle. You may be a woman.

FORWARD (For Women Only)

Let's start with all you men who thought that you would just be thorough and go ahead and read this section too. What's the matter with you?? Read the sign! For Women Only! Do you go around wandering into ladies' restrooms too?

Look, man, I'm just happy that you're going to read this book at all. That's thorough enough. But there is nothing in this section for you. Seriously. Give your wife some space and get out of here. Go to the Introduction. Now!

Okay, Ladies... This entire book is a sort of boys' club. In it we're going to talk about manly stuff in manly ways. You wouldn't like it in the same way you don't like your husband's favorite t-shirt – it's gross and ugly and makes him look slobby, but if he likes it it's not really worth a fight. It's the same kind of thing here. But before you leave it to him, we need to talk.

I am a husband of fifteen years and a father of three kids. So I know a little bit about who calls the shots in the family. And in my family it's not always me. I know that you ladies wield a significant amount (okay, most!) of the power when it comes to the family. You do, I admit it, and surprise-surprise, I'm okay with it. Why wouldn't I be? You ladies have a built-in hard-wired advantage over us – maternal instinct. It's a powerful thing and we can't compete with it. Have you noticed that no one ever talks about "paternal instinct"? That's because paternal instinct says things like "she can go a few more hours in that diaper" and "it's okay to give the baby a sip of beer". So even though we don't say it, you're in charge. We need you around and we're happy that you're here because, frankly, we want the kids to live.

But... See how I did that? I complimented you and made you feel good, but now I'm going to say something stupid to ruin it. Typical male. But... just because your maternal instinct gave you a running start on us does not mean that we can't catch up. Or that we don't want to. And that's a point worth making.

There's this image of men out there, mostly in sitcoms, that we are overweight, clueless schlubs. We're incorrigible! But goshdarnit, even if it looks like we slept with our secretary but it was just a kooky mix up or we burned the house down because we were sneaking cigars in bed, at the end of the day we're just too adorable for you to live without. The only good news for you in this sitcom scenario is that you are young and super hot. We don't deserve you.

Another type of male exists in parenting books. This is the New Dad. The New Dad is completely flipped out. He barfed when he heard you were pregnant, he whines that he may never get to have sex again, and he is scared to death of the baby. In short, New Dad is a pussy (sorry, sometimes the right word is just the right word). However, the good news is that, like the Sitcom Dad, I don't believe that New Dad actually exists. And here's why. Because I don't think any of you ladies would marry these men and make babies with them!

Here in the real world, all of my friends are normal guys with normal wives. They have hopes and fears for their kids, but they basically try to have a good time with the process. What they (and I) lack is information. You have magazines and TV shows and your mothers and mommy groups with each other for information on how to be a good mom. We have nothing. We don't talk to each other about stuff like that. And last time I checked, Parents magazine didn't have a swimsuit issue, so we're not reading that either. But this book – yes, this book - is the thing.

I mentioned before that I am a regular guy with three kids. I am not a doctor and I have no parental training. But through some miracle I am a great dad. Not good. Great. It happened

You Are Going To Get Poop On You

because over time I developed a parenting strategy based on two things and only two things: discipline and respect. Through that strategy I realized that my children's upbringing was not just a product of my wife's influence on them. I had developed dad-centric information and taken an active place in there too. My kids were better off because of my involvement, and so were my wife and I. And this, Ladies, is why you want your husbands to read this book.

Let me be clear, this book is entertaining and funny, so you don't have to feel bad about buying it for him. But wrapped in that entertainment is a parenting philosophy specifically for dads. I've used it on my own kids, so I know that it works. It will work for your husband too.

But the best part is that once he reads and starts applying what he knows, he will have information – about himself and the kids. You want him to have that information because it opens up a dialogue between the two of you about parenting. Without it, the older the kids get, the farther behind he falls, and the harder that dialogue becomes. He needs this information now.

So I offer you <u>You Are Going To Get Poop On You</u>. It works for me – a certified non-genius. It will work for him. And, by extension, you.

So that's it, Ladies; your part here is done. Just hand the book over to your husband. And if he complains about it, just point to the back of the book and the quote from David Zucker and remind him that David wrote Airplane! If David Zucker thinks it's funny, then it's funny!

Once you've done that, your part in our story ends. Know that I thank you and you've done all you can to help our hero find his way. Now stop reading. There is nothing for you beyond here except your husband's favorite t-shirt.

And guys, if you read this, boooooooooooooooooooo on you. I hope that your kids follow instructions better than you do. But this next part is for you, so here we go...

INTRODUCTION

"And THIS book says that you should stop crying."

When my son was four years old he started to use the word "dammit". Like all the time. Now I don't know what a four-year old has to curse about, much less damn. It's not like his team lost the Super Bowl or he stepped on a Lego or one of his kids took off her diaper and made a little modern art on the wall. Those are dammits. But whatever it was, he was definitely feeling it. Luke can't find his shoe? "Dammit!" Luke has to take a bath? "Dammit!" Luke has to leave a playdate at his friend's house while his friend's parents are watching and judging me?

"DAMMIT!"

So here I was with a cussing four-year old. One thing I know for sure is that he got it from me. What can I say? The baby spilled my beer? "Dammit!" I stubbed my toe on the chair? "Dammit!" The idiot in the car in front of me won't go even though the light has been green for over two seconds? "DAMMIT!" No question, I am to blame. Of course, then my son moved on to "What the…??", which he may have gotten from me, but I don't think so. I usually finish that sentence. I think he got that one from SpongeBob.

I don't tell you any of this to illustrate what a foulmouth I am. Because I'm not. I'm just like you. Actually, check that. I'm worse than you. I'm sure you're special in some way. You can play chopsticks on the piano or juggle or pick your nose with your tongue. I can't do any of those things. I'm regular. Average. No more, no less. But as a more-or-less average guy, I follow certain guidelines. One of those is: when I'm going to spend my time reading an advice book, I would at least like to get that advice from someone who is actually like me.

Here's how I see it – if there's something wrong with my car, I want to talk to a guy who has a car like mine who has had a similar problem with it. What I don't want is to talk to NASCAR superstar Rusty Wallace about it. See? I mean, call me crazy, but I don't ask Tiger Woods about golf.

"Hey, Tig, what do you do if you hammer-slice your ball into the street and it smashes through the windshield of a passing car?"

"Well, Joe, I either run away or blame the group playing behind me. But either way I never play that course again."

I also don't ask Donald Trump about money.

"Hey, Don—"

"It's Donald."

You Are Going To Get Poop On You

"Whatever. I have about three thousand dollars. What do you suggest I do with it?"

"How about a wallet. Or a money clip?"

Experts don't understand us or what we're going through. Sure they write a lot of books. But they don't understand that we have limited time and resources. So they can't see that their fifty-three-step plan to cure our kids and us in one weekend just isn't going to work. Which leaves the only other group who writes books like this – celebrities.

Celebrities may seem normal, but they're not. I know that they write a lot of books like this and they're all light and funny and whatever. But the problem with celebrities is they don't know anything. They don't raise their kids. They have mountains of money and round-the-clock nannies. Oh sure, their kids have interesting, original names and end up in magazines a lot, but that hardly qualifies as practical parenting advice.

So it's not a great situation. Experts have too much information, celebrities have too little, and all we know for sure is what we don't want – a fancy explanation, or a chart, or a footnote, or, for the love of all things decent and holy, a woman's take on it. No, we want counsel from regular people like us. But the problem with that is that we're men. So we're likely not to ask anyone at all, even if we feel like we really should. So I guess we're stuck, right? Not anymore.

But before I get too far, let's look at you. You're a man, and here you are with this book. It's safe to assume that there's something going on in your life that caused you to have it. Hey, I get it. Times are tough. If you're a new dad (or going to be) maybe you're wondering how you'll make the adjustment. There's money, time, space, and tons of baby stuff to consider. Maybe the economy is causing you to make some changes.

According to recent Department of Labor statistics, men are affected by unemployment at twice the rate of women. Maybe your wife is going to work and you're going to stay home (which is how it is for me). It's happening: In the last ten years the number of stay-at-home dads has tripled in the U.S. If you're already a dad, those same things can affect you too.

Or maybe when it comes to your kids you're just lost. Maybe you're afraid of your kids. Maybe you're henpecked. Maybe your mother-in-law is involved (ooh, I hope that's not it) or maybe you just think your wife knows more than you do about this stuff. I mean, she reads Parents magazine, right? Like I said, I get it. So now you're fighting back. And you're wondering what I think. Well... I think you had better know whom you're asking.

Who in the hell is Joe Reilly?

I mentioned before that I am a regular guy. I'm not a scientist or a doctor or a priest or a teacher or a behavioral therapist or anything. I'm not trained in any way. I'm not even much of a writer. BUT... I am a great dad.

I'm not saying that I love my kids and they love me, even though that's true. No, I'm saying that I'm great at being a dad in the same way that Wayne Gretzky is great at hockey. He was just born with it. So was I. I see the big picture. I get kids and they get me. I've actually had people bring their kids to spend time with me. That's crazy, right?

Because I'm nothing special. I like hamburgers better than steak, Hershey over Ghirardelli, and Bud over Heineken. I play video games, watch football, and am fascinated by Navy SEALs. For my entire adult life I've either been overweight or on Weight Watchers. And I'm susceptible to everything. If there's a flu going around, I get it. If it's rainy, I'm depressed. I'm incredibly fearful of drugs because I just know that I would be one of those worst case scenario stories, trying to sell my kids' Lincoln Logs for my next fix. What else? Oh, I say f**k and s**t in front of people (including kids) way more than I should. Remember Luke and his "dammits"? Don't worry, I have a reason for telling you all this.

My brother, when he was dating, had a thing he would do when he started going out with a girl he really liked. He would sit her down and tell her every awful, humiliating story he could think of about himself. It seems like a bad idea, but it was smart. The girl would know exactly with whom she was getting together, and, more importantly, he would beat the rest of the family to the punch. By the time we got there, she had already heard about the time he drove into a tree or slept naked in his own barf in the bushes. I'm giving you a little bit of the same thing here, but I'm still a great dad. Which was a realization that sort of snuck up on me.

One day I was complaining to a friend of mine on the phone about how I wanted more money, like right now. His response was, "Joe, what about love?" So I hung up on him. But after he called back I joked with him that I was all full up on love and that I'd be willing to trade some of it for some money. Then I realized that what I was saying was true. Thanks to my wife and kids, I'm pretty full up on love. I do not know where it came from and I sure didn't expect it, and that's the God's honest truth. Because I have a terrible foundation when it comes to family life.

I have terrible parents. No joke. It took me a long time to realize that and even longer to say it out loud. My parents weren't drunks or beaters or molesters or anything like that. With my parents, I don't know what the condition is called, but they hated us. I'm the oldest of four kids, and I don't mean that my parents hated the way we acted. I mean they hated us and wished us harm. They fed us and clothed us and let us live in the house, and, to the outside world, everything looked fine (which is part of the pathology). But inside our house it was psychological warfare 24/7. You'd wake up in bed and someone would literally be standing over you telling you what a scumbag you were. And you were eleven years old. It was freaky.

I remember my mom throwing a TV at my dad. He walked in, asked her a question during a show, and she sped over to the TV, which was about the size of a beachball, whipped the cord out of the wall and, screaming like an animal, heaved the whole thing at him. It smashed on the tile floor and my dad just laughed, trying to push her over the top. It was weird that he laughed at that.

One time, my brother borrowed my car for a few hours. A car that I had been driving for three years without incident. Somehow he completely burned up the engine. It was locked up – frozen solid. So he comes home and tells my parents that I didn't refill the car with oil and that burned up the engine. I was instantly the biggest A-hole on the planet. But seriously? Give me a break! Cars don't suddenly run out of oil and lock up! When does that happen? Plus, my dad was an engineer. A mechanical engineer! Surely he knew that cars don't act like that! As I recall, we both got into trouble.

I've had my birthday skipped more than once, I've been told that I and every friend I ever had was a loser, and I have been granted and denied requests for no reason other than to watch me or one of my siblings squirm. As I write this it sounds insignificant. But when you're young and every move, no matter how small – what you eat, how you greet someone when they enter a room, anything – can cause a volcanic eruption, it wears on you. Over time you become gun shy, and you blame yourself.

But now we're WAY off the subject. I'm only telling you

all this to show you that I have no foundation for great parenting. I have no instincts that I trust. You know those people on shows like Survivor who get a chance to see their moms and just dissolve? I don't have that and I don't get that, but I want that for my kids. And that's the reason that I wrote this book.

What I saw was that my kids have a much better relationship with me (at least for now) than I ever had with my parents, and I wanted to put into words how I thought that had happened. I wanted to be able, at some later date, to give this to them as a tool that they could use with their own families. So I took a look at what I was doing with them, and realized that I had a definite parenting philosophy.

Your Parenting Philosophy

Let me ask you this: What is your philosophy on investing? How about politics? Or driving a car? Or golf? You can answer those questions pretty easily I bet. You probably have philosophies on many many things, and, when people ask you about one of them, you can talk clearly about it. But try this: What is your philosophy on parenting? Most men don't have one. At least, not one that they can easily articulate. There's something wrong with that, considering how much time we spend doing it and how invested we are. But we're here to change that. It's why you're reading the book.

When I looked at my kids and what I was doing with them, I realized that, along with my wife, I was employing a simple and continuous philosophy of **discipline and respect**. Now I didn't develop this method and then try it out on my kids. I did the opposite. I realized that my kids were turning out better than I or anyone else in my family ever had, and I wondered why. I had no reason to believe that they would turn out so well, and I certainly wasn't under the delusion that I was a parenting genius, so I worked backward and tried to discover how they got that way.

What I found out was that, by using a combination of discipline and respect with my kids, it took our relationship beyond that of the normal parent and child. I was more effective with them, and they we're more attuned to me. It was surprising because I hadn't thought it out before. It was just happening.

My first reaction to my self-analysis was, "Oh yeah! I am a parenting genius!" Which lasted about five seconds before reality set in. Obviously, what I was doing wasn't hard or I wouldn't be doing it. Duh. On top of that, if it was hard I wouldn't be able to use it on the kids. So, "I'm a parenting genius" quickly became "I'm a parenting...normal...I guess."

Another thing that brought my non-geniosity (just one of many fancy words I know) home was I realized that, while the discipline/respect thing was working, and working well, it wasn't perfect. Because my kids aren't perfect and I'm not perfect. But that's okay. Even though my philosophy wasn't perfect, and even though it was still nutty old me at the controls, it was working well enough. And you know what? Most times, good enough is good enough. So I sat down and wrote about it.

I worked at soccer practices, piano lessons, in the car, at home in front of SpongeBob, and anywhere else I could get some peace. I was committed to it because I thought it was important. Because I was writing this for my kids, and for me. But, lucky you, they're not all that interested yet. So you're up!

And it's time to get started. You've heard way more about my inner workings than I wanted you to, and you already know more about me than 90% of my friends. But the point is clear (I hope): If I can do it, you can do it. Also, if I feel like it's worth doing even though I like my hobbies and my lazy weekends, then you probably will, too. But judge for yourself. Feel free to read any or all (or none) of this book. Maybe you'll read what I have to say and do the opposite. Hey, I'm not very scientific. But neither is a hammer, and a hammer gets the job done just fine. I'm happy to be an unscientific hammer. Because all I know and all I care about is what works. I have three kids and a happy wife. We have the stress of jobs and money and too little space, but the family works.

Finally, I'm not special at anything. Not one thing. Who is? The good news is you don't have to be either – and that includes reading. This is going to be a short book. Who wants to spend their off time reading and being told what to do by some know-it-all writer? Exactly. No one. So I've set the bar pretty low.

I have a friend who only reads books with "big words and thick pages" and I'm hoping that he'll read this book. So going forward let's keep it big and thick. And remember, it doesn't matter what we do, it just has to work.

JOE REILLY

Chapter 1 – PRE-PREGNANCY
A.K.A. THE LAST TIME YOU'LL BE IN CONTROL OF THIS PROCESS
FOR ABOUT A YEAR

"Honey! Have you seen my hammer?"

This is not a book about pregnancy. There are a million of those already. Besides, pregnancy is easy for us. I even gained about thirty pounds of "sympathy weight" during my wife's first pregnancy. Believe me, thirty pounds in nine months doesn't come from hard living. This is a book about raising kids. But since being a dad starts with pregnancy (in most cases), it's worth mentioning a few things from the man's perspective. Speaking of which…

Ladies, this is your last chance to get out of here. This is a book for men. So if you're a woman, put it down. Men, don't let your wives read over your shoulders. They won't get it and they'll be mad at you for reading it because you won't be taking something seriously that's important to the well-being of the new family and blah and blah and blah. Not only will they not think that this will make you a better dad, they're going to think this is going to make you a worse husband. Like that's even possible! Right? High five? No? Ahem…

Okay, Ladies, you were warned.

Be careful what you wish for

Two things in this life that if you get them you had damn sure better have wanted them are (1) a wife and (2) kids. There's no way around this one. You have to recently and in all honesty have said, "I want to be married" and "I want to have kids". There's a reason for this. You may not believe it now, especially if you're a newlywed or don't have kids yet, but at some point in your marriage/fatherhood you're going to go so far off the deep end that you're going to want to burn your family tree to the ground and dig up its roots so that it can never grow to harm anyone else ever again. On that day you HAVE to be able to look in the mirror and say to yourself, "Well, crap. I said I wanted this". It doesn't get any more fundamental than that.

The only problem with saying "I want marriage/I want kids" is that women will jump at that. They're looking for guys who say things like that. Then before you know it, your wish has come true. You have a wife and a baby and absolutely no idea what to do with either one of them. There's no training for us in this. No college course, no magazines, no TV shows. Women get all this info from their mothers. It's good heartfelt advice and they get it whenever they want for the rest of their lives. But dads? No. Dads are brutal in this arena.

Dadvice

I don't really remember the first (and only) sex talk I had with my dad, but I remember that my ears were really hot and I felt like I might be getting an instant case of diarrhea. All I do remember is my dad listing every word he could think of to describe an erection. Boner, hard on, stiffy, rod, dick, pole. It just went on and on for what must have been hours. To this day I have no idea what I was supposed to have learned from that talk except that my dad would run the table on that category on Jeopardy! "I'll take Every Name In The World for a Cock for $500, Alex."

My brother-in-law didn't even get the talk from his dad. He got it from his mom. My mother-in-law took him out of the house into the garage and explained to him in about five minutes what sex was all about. What he came away with was that a really super-hard red rod comes out of the man's penis and hurts everyone. Badly.

These are the explanations we get on a subject that we like. I like sex! I assume that my dad did, too. And this is what I get? So when it comes to marriage and kids, which are way more complicated and a lot less fun, the explanations just don't come at all. So how do we NOT make mistakes? The answer is we don't. We screw up across the board.

Pick the right wife

Do you want one way to avoid child-rearing mistakes? Pick the right wife. I'm not kidding. I know that it sounds a lot like a line from one of my favorite movies, Bull Durham: "Baseball is a simple game. You hit the ball, you catch the ball, you throw the ball." But it's true; that's the essence of the game. So pick the right wife. She'll cover up a lot of your inadequacies in the parenting area. Trust me, your wife can make you a better dad. She'll teach you things, you'll be able to bounce ideas off her, and you'll present a united front to your kids. But she's also going to lean on you. Not in a bad way. But she's human, so she'll get tired, angry, depressed, and everything you get. So you'd better like her. You'll never be able to handle the kids if you're at odds with your wife. Find the right wife before you make the baby.

Making the baby

So you said, "I want to be married," and you picked out a good wife. Then you decided, "Oh what the hell. I want a baby. At least it will get the old lady off my back." Or something equally romantic. So you figured out when the right time of the month is. You made dinner and had some wine. Now you're ready to make a baby, which you know how to do because you had the boner talk with your dad. But what you may not know is that making a baby can be hard.

I don't know what the girls were taught, but it's not like we were taught. By the time I was about thirteen I thought that if I got my penis anywhere near a woman - not just near her vagina, near her ear! – that she would get pregnant 110% of the time. With twins. That, combined with my Catholic upbringing where anything that smacks of premarital sex is a sin, had me pretty convinced that I was a baby making machine sent here to earth from the bowels of hell to ruin some poor girl's life because she was in the same room with my all-powerful phallus. Needless to say, when my wife told me it was time to have a baby (isn't that how it goes for most of us), I was looking nine months ahead to the birth. Reality check: it took us three years to make our daughter. But it wasn't for lack of trying.

I used to play rec league ice hockey. It was reasonably serious. You get drafted and there are playoffs and trophies for the winners and all that. Several of my friends had been in the league for a while, some for as many as ten years, but none had ever won a trophy. So my first year in the league I win a trophy.

Then for the next four years I win trophies again. Five trophies in five seasons! My friends still had none unless they'd played a season on my team. I was rolling. But then my team moved up to the A League.

The A League had several minor league hockey players in it, and I played one game and realized that I wasn't good enough to stay. So I was released and quickly snapped up by a new team. And by the time the regular season was done we had the best record in the league. So now I'm thinking, "Wow, I could win six trophies in six seasons with two different teams. I am a hockey god!" But it wasn't meant to be. We lost in the semifinals of the playoffs in double overtime. I was physically exhausted, spiritually crushed, it was after midnight and I had to work the next day. So I get home and my wife has timed it out perfectly. Welcome home, Stud. Time to make a baby. I have to tell you, I never wanted to have sex less in my entire life. But I did it. I think it took about an hour and a half, and I kept thinking about the game-winning goal over and over, but I did it. And after all that, did we make a baby that night? No.

Just know that if you're trying to have kids, it can be hard. It seems like everyone in the world has a kid. Teenagers are getting pregnant all over the place. There's a woman at the grocery store with seven kids and food stamps, and you have a job and can't even make one damn baby! Hang in there. There's a grand plan. Besides, you've already cleared the biggest hurdle. You went against all reasonable judgment and said, "I want to have a baby".

My boys can swim

I've had the pleasure of having my wife get pregnant on three different occasions, and each one was very different. With my first daughter we found out at my in-laws' house. They were having a pool party and my wife went to the bathroom and peed on the pregnancy test stick and it came up with two lines. Two lines! Oh my god, two lines! She showed it to me and we showed it to her parents who showed it to their friends. The whole party celebrated and we basked in the glow of familial love and approval.

Two years later for my son, we found out in our apartment. It was three a.m. and my wife woke me up and dragged me into the bathroom. She was jumping for joy. She had peed on the stick again and, yet again, we got the blessed two lines. But there was no one around and it was three a.m. so I said, "Babe, I'm so happy. This is awesome. Will you be mad if I go back to bed now?" Not exactly the celebration we had for our daughter.

Four years after that I was sitting in the living room reading to the kids when my wife stormed into the room. She came right for me, jammed a pregnancy test in my face, and tapped her toe waiting for my response. I looked and said, "Oh. Two lines? Really?" She didn't say anything. She stared right into my soul with eyes that said, "Look what you did to me!" and she stormed out of the room again. After that we had a two day fight about whose fault this was.

But no matter how your wife gets pregnant or how unreasonably she takes it, she (and you) are going to feel the urge to spread the news. When we had our son (baby number two) we decided to just live with the news for a day. Just the two of us knew and we just savored it. Then we called people and started all of the hullabaloo. I have to say that that one day was brilliant. It is one of my best memories of my wife's pregnancy because it was just us on our own, not answering questions, and just feeling good. You don't get a lot of days like that. Take it if you can. Because soon your wife will start to undergo some serious physical and emotional changes.

You, however, aren't changing at all.

Chapter 1 – The Wrap-Up
 1. Want to have kids before you have kids.

2. Making a baby can be easy or hard, planned or a surprise. Either way, be the man and roll with it.

Chapter 2 – SO YOU'RE GONNA BE A DAD

"Where did he learn the F word?"
"Uh...Preschool?"

The Pregnancy

Here are some interesting facts about your wife's pregnancy:

- Her blood volume will increase by 50%.
- She will gain weight.
- Her boobs will look like full size Nerf footballs.
- She will have hormones galore running through her body.
- As a result of the hormones she will love you and

loathe you, hug you and hit you, want you and reject you, all on a minute-by-minute basis.
- Food she used to love will make her vomit just to smell it.
- Her hands and feet may swell to the point that they don't look like her own anymore.
- She will have to pee all the time.
- Her hair may fall out.
- Her belly button will pop out like the button on a cooked turkey.
- And on and on and on.

Now here are some interesting facts about the pregnancy for you:

- Nothing. You don't change a bit.

So while you're wife is undergoing a total physical, spiritual, and emotional overhaul, you are still going to work, emailing your friends, and wondering how your fantasy football team could be sucking so badly. Your wife is developing a connection with the baby and, even though she and others may be asking and putting pressure on you, you're not. But don't feel bad if you don't feel any different. Why should you? Besides, you will feel different later anyway.

Months 0-3

This is not the best time I ever had. As we already covered, your wife is changing all over the place, but she's not changing enough for her liking. The first thing that comes is the morning sickness. This is when your wife is in the middle of something – eating, shopping, sleeping – and goes and barfs, and then continues doing whatever she was doing before she barfed. Morning sickness had different levels of intensity for each of our kids, but it was always immediate, always gross, and never in the morning. I don't even think my wife could explain what set it off. Then after about three months you look at each other and have your usual daily dinner-table conversation, "Did you barf today?"

"No. I haven't barfed since Tuesday!" And just like that it's over. It's kind of like a headache or a mouth sore that way. It really sucks for a while and then it's just gone, and you didn't even realize.

What doesn't happen during this three months is any physical sign that your wife is having a baby. She'll spend a lot of time weighing herself and standing sideways in the mirror to see if she appears pregnant. She'll ask you all the time if she looks pregnant, which gets really annoying. Especially since she'll ask during the last two minutes of any NFL game, or during March Madness, or while you're asleep. Also, if she's competitive at all, she'll hate on people who are more pregnant than she is. "You know my friend, Alice?

"Alice that was maid of honor at our wedding? Your sorority sister?"

"Yeah, she thinks she's so great just because she has to wear maternity clothes. But I think she just looks like a fat pig bitch." It's probably just the hormones talking, but just be ready. She just wants the world to know what's happening to her.

Months 4-6

During this time, things are actually pretty good. It has been a few months, so you and your wife are used to her being pregnant. The morning sickness is over, and, thank God, your wife's body is starting to match her disposition. People see her and comment, "Oh, you're having a baby! Your first?" This is followed by a twenty minute conversation between your wife and whatever stranger made the comment while you stand there in the grocery store or parking lot or street corner nodding and saying, "Uh huh." But it's okay because it's a little exciting; plus your wife is happy.

Another thing that makes your wife happy is, if she has any friends at all there will be parties. Now I never went to any of these parties because they conflicted with...anything, but my wife always had fun and came home with something diaper or boob related, which is fun.

This is also a time when your wife may be able to stand your presence again. Not only are the hormones more under control, they actually, depending on how you look at it, work in your favor. Which is to say you may get to have sex again. Don't count on it, and don't get mad if you don't get it. Remember all the changes she's going through? So don't hold it against her if she doesn't want to add your junk to the mix. Besides, it's sort of a good news/bad news situation anyway. On the plus side, you can touch your wife without her puking or cussing you out and pointing you toward the Playboy channel. The flip side is she's all...different, and you may not want to touch her.

I had this both ways. Sometimes I found my wife's big boobs and round belly sexy. Other times not so much. And I'll be honest here, it was mostly not so much. I mean, come on, if pregnant women looked so great then Larry Flynt would have put out Pregnant Hustler by now. But it is the only sex you're going to get, so just keep telling her she looks great and whichever way it goes for you, don't worry about it. It's all about making her happy at this stage anyway, and anything you get is just a bonus.

Months 7-9

By now your wife is huge. Like orca fat. Or soon will be. Her giant boobs lay flat on top of her planetoid-shaped belly. Her internal organs have all been mashed up into her throat as the baby gets bigger and takes up more room. The woman of your dreams is now a mere shadow of her former self. Oh sure, you're still telling her that she looks good – MUCH better than those other pregnant cows – but you still can't believe what you're seeing. I mean, she's going to get back to normal, right?

She can't sleep or get comfortable anywhere. She has heartburn, and if you're really lucky, hemorrhoids. It seems like everything is out of place, and beginning at the end of month eight she will start letting you know on an hourly basis that (1) she is miserable and (2) she can't do this. And by "do this" she means deliver the baby.

Needless to say, month nine sucks. Across the board my wife was miserable in month nine. And her misery made everyone miserable. All you can do is man up and live through it. There's no point in arguing with her. She knows that she is pissing you off, but she doesn't care because she has the trump card – she's carrying the baby. And any conversation about whether she can do this is pointless. She knows that whether she can do it or not, she's having this baby. She's just scared to be having an eight pound, twenty inch long human being rip its way through a very sensitive two-inch hole. She just wants you to sympathize and say something like, "I know, babe. You're going to be the best mom ever." As opposed to, "I'm glad I'm not a woman! That is going to suck. But I hope your vagina doesn't get too messed up though." See the difference?

It's going to suck, a lot, but you don't have that much longer to go.

Dr. Doctor, give me the news

Up to this point your wife will have been to a dozen or so appointments with her OB/GYN. Hopefully, you will have been able to attend a few of these as well. This is your kid and we don't live in the fifties. You don't get to hang outside with all the other dudes in fedoras smoking Pall Malls. But another reason for you to go to the appointments is to keep an eye on the doctor.

We had different OBs for each of our kids' births. We loved our first guy, Dr. Johnson. He was good-looking and cool and totally calm about everything. He also drove a motorcycle. He used words like "perfect" and "ideal" and "wonderful" all the time, and we had a flawless experience with him. But because of insurance (m****r f*****s!) we had to switch OBs for our next baby, and we ended up with Dr. Rapoza.

Dr. Rapoza was also a good guy and we had a good experience. He was no Dr. Johnson, but he was no Dr. Frankenstein either. But by the time we had our third baby we had to switch doctors again. Thanks, insurance industry!

This time we ended up with Dr. Rubin, and this is the part of this chapter where you need to pay attention. For Dr. Rubin, this was a job. And she wasn't paying very close attention to it. She didn't use words like "perfect" and "wonderful", and I was getting a bad vibe off of her. We had been through this before and we were rereading all our pregnancy books, so we knew pretty much what to do when. So we'd go in for an appointment and my wife would say, "Shouldn't I be having a glucose test right about now?" And Dr. Rubin would look at us and then be like, "Oh yeah." "Oh yeah??" WTF, Dr. Rubin??

This went on for several appointments until finally my wife asked a biggie. "When are you going to give me the triple marker?" The triple marker is a blood test that is used to screen for spina bifida, Down syndrome, and other chromosome disorders. It is usually given between weeks 15 and 18 of the pregnancy. There's another test called a CVS that is given around week 12, but we had passed on that one because insurance doesn't cover it (thank you, insurance!) and we knew that we could always do the triple marker. The only problem was that my wife asked the question in week 26.

Dr. Rubin had totally fanned on administering that test and now we were entering the third trimester of the pregnancy. The test could still be performed, but if the baby was at risk for Down syndrome or anencephaly (which is the absence of a large part of the brain and skull) or anything else, there was nothing we could do about it. Late-term abortions are highly controversial at best and illegal at worst.

Now before you judge me as a fetus eating Hitler-demon, let's be clear. I didn't want an abortion, I didn't order an abortion, I didn't get an abortion. I do not support abortion, and I am now really sick of the word abortion. But the whole reason that the triple marker is given by week 18 is so that families who can't or don't want to have a baby who is in some way challenged can terminate the pregnancy. Believe what you want, but I'm just telling you why doctors do what they do. And what Dr. Rubin did by not paying attention was take that option away from us.

When she finally did administer the test and the results came back, our baby was right on the line – not at risk, but not in the clear. Then Dr. Rubin made matters worse. In order to cover her ass, she brought in her boss who tried to bully us. He told us that this was not Dr. Rubin's fault and that we should just move on because there was nothing wrong and there was nothing we could do about it anyway. I told him to shut his fat mouth and perform an amniocentesis right there right that second. An amniocentesis (amnio) extracts fetal DNA which can be examined, and I wanted to know. Dr. Boss Bullyman huffed around and finally tried to do the amnio, but because of where the baby and the placenta were located there was no way to do it without serious risk to the baby or my wife. So that meeting ended with me making it very clear to Dr. Rubin's boss that if we delivered a surprise baby with Down syndrome or no head, I was going to own his practice. So for the next three months, right up until ten seconds after my daughter was born, we were wondering if she was going to be okay.

The moral to this story, men, is this: Pay attention to your doctors. They're human and they make mistakes. I know that they're doctors and you're just an electrician, but this is your kid. Don't be afraid to bust the doctors' balls even if you might be wrong.

*Holy f*****g s**t! The baby is coming!*

So you made it through the whole nine months and your wife tells you that the baby is coming. The first thing to know here is that it's not like it is in the movies. If it were a movie this whole thing would start with your wife's water breaking. You'd be walking down some boardwalk and enjoying an ice cream cone – one cone between the two of you – and not even thinking about the baby. You'd be playing some witty palindrome word game and then water would splash all over the boardwalk like your wife got hit in the groin with a water balloon. Then she would be rushed to the hospital and after pushing twice would deliver the baby in five minutes. But this is not a movie.

In reality you'll be at home because your wife is too miserable to move. You'll be watching TV because you've run out of things to talk about. You'll each have your own ice cream because she's not about to share with you after you did this to her. And your wife's water won't break at all because that rarely happens. In all three pregnancies the nurses at the hospital broke my wife's water for her.

What will probably happen is that your wife will go, "Ooh! I think that was a contraction." Then you'll jump up like a mad man and start packing, thinking it's time to go to the hospital. It's not. Especially if this is your first baby. With our first daughter my wife started contractions on a Tuesday and the baby was delivered on Thursday. In the meantime I stayed up for forty straight hours and started hallucinating. So you have time.

The hospital

Eventually, though, the contractions will be coming at the right intervals and intensity and you will go to the hospital. And there you will wait. They'll get your wife situated, take her blood pressure, monitor her contractions, and generally wait around until the baby is ready. Again, if this is your first baby feel free to pace and stress and watch the monitors. It's sort of a rite of passage. But when you're having your second baby, you'll leave your wife in the room and gather with the other multiple-time dads or even the nurses and make fun of the pacing, sweaty first-timers.

Now I know that we live in this world where men are in touch with their feminine sides and we think that the birth of the child is sacred and we're a team and all that. I mean, we can't believe that just thirty/forty years ago our dads totally missed our births because they were getting their hair cut, right? But even today I still lean a little more that way. I don't know, maybe I'm a little more Cro-Magnon than I should be, but I can tell you that after three births, interest wanes.

When I was waiting for my youngest to be born, I decided to go get tires for the car. My wife was cool with it. I mean, it's just another baby, right? So the car was up on the platform and I was enjoying my double-double In-N-Out burger when my phone rang. It was the nurse from the hospital telling me to get my ass back there right now! So I had to wolf down my burger, cancel the tires, and go back. I felt a little put out at the time, and I was definitely mad at the nurse, but my daughter was born about an hour after I got back. So it would have been close. At least it would have been more like the movies.

More doctors

Remember our little talk about doctors earlier? The same applies here. The only difference is it's nurses and the occasional anesthesiologist now. In fact, if your experience is anything like ours was, you won't even see your wife's doctor until about one minute before the baby is born.

When both my son and daughter were born the nurses actually asked us if we wanted to wait for the doctor. I guess the baby was right there and the doctor wasn't, so why not get things moving? In both cases we waited. Just know that you're in charge. If you want to have the baby, have it. If you want to wait for the doctor, then wait. But be aware of what's going on.

Before my first daughter was born we had a perfectly well-meaning nurse preparing to break my wife's water after another nurse had already done it. My wife was ready to deliver the baby and the nurse was about to poke it with a sharp stick. So we gently, but firmly set her straight. When my other daughter was born we had a doctor who wasn't managing my wife's pain very well (in my opinion). He was being stingy with the epidural medicine and my wife was starting to freak out. On top of that no one could find him. So I walked all over that hospital and found him. Then I walked him back to my wife and told him that if he didn't fix this right now he was going to have a six-foot, two-hundred-and-ten pound problem called Joe Reilly. Was I way out of line? Yeah, probably. Did I apologize later? Yes. But did my outburst get him off his ass and solve my wife's problem. And how!

As a new dad, you've got a little license when it comes to the delivery. Everyone knows that you're having a baby and you are stressed out. So use that to your advantage. You are in charge. Threaten to slap, stab or bite whomever you want. If you apologize later all will be forgiven.

The actual birth

Again, this could not be any less like the movies. In the movies your wife is in the bed in the operating room and a team of doctors monitors her condition. You all wear masks and gowns and your wife sweats beautifully as she pushes out the perfect pink baby. Then you take your new baby out into the hall for everyone in your family to meet. That's the movie version. By comparison, the actual version is almost surreal.

First, there is no private operating room. The room that you're in is the room where your wife is having the baby. It doesn't look anything like an operating room. It looks like a living room. Your baby is about to be born in the living room. Also, the door is wide open and your wife's privates are pointing right at it. There's no privacy at all! Anyone who walks by and looks in – and a lot of people do – will get a good look at your wife's vagina. So that's a little unsettling. Then there are the clothes. There are no masks or gowns or anything. You just stand there in your hockey jersey and cargo shorts ready to catch the baby. Even the doctors are totally informal about the dress code. One of our doctors delivered the baby in a leather motorcycle outfit. Sometimes – and this happened with all three kids – you'll be in the middle of pushing and breathing and baby delivering, and you'll realize that there's no one else in the room. It's just you and your wife! Nurses and doctors just wander in and out like it's a Starbucks.

Then at some point the baby will be ready and everyone will start paying attention. This is when the pushing starts. I don't have a lot to say in this area because my wife was a champion pusher. In fact, when we had our first daughter my wife pushed so well that the nurses asked her to stop so that they could go get some nurse trainees and show them how the pushing was supposed to be done. No kidding. Right in the middle of becoming a mother, my wife had to stop and illustrate proper pushing technique.

In the end, though, she pushed a few times and blam, the baby came out. That was pretty standard for all our kids. My wife said Get Out and they got out. Not all women are so lucky. Some push for hours. And hours. And hours. Sometimes the doctor has to go in there with the tongs and pull the baby out. Sometimes it has to be a C-Section. But when the baby does come, DON'T LOOK. You will anyway, but at least you can say it was your own fault. "No no, I shouldn't have looked. Joe warned me."

The doctors and nurses make it hard not to look. There are mirrors that they keep angling so you can see better, and they keep moving you down toward your wife's crotch. You have to make an effort not to look. The first reason is that you don't want to see your wife's vagina in this state.

Remember that time when you were in the cabin in the woods or at the beach just after sunset and there was a fire and you and your wife got naked and you looked at her vagina and it was perfect? It put those Playboy girls to shame! Well right now, as this baby is making its way into the world, say goodbye to that vagina. Because right now it looks like it just went up against Frank Dux in the Kumite.

I'll admit, I looked. What can I say, I didn't have a badass book like this to tell me any different. Want to know what I saw? I saw a package of Eckrich smoked sausage covered in blood with a blood-covered baseball sitting in the gap between the two sausages. And to this day that is what I see because my brain will not translate the horror into actual reality. But hey, you want to look? Go ahead.

The second reason you don't look is the baby itself. Remember the movie baby? This baby is the alien that kills the movie baby. When your baby comes out it is covered in blood, mucous, and white crap called vernix. Also, it is not pink or shaped right. The baby is red if anything, but may be yellow or blue. I know you're laughing and you think that I'm kidding, but I'm not. Your baby might be yellow. It could even be brown if your wife poops on the table, which happens (not to my wife, though). The shape problem is a function of all the pushing and if the doctor had to do any pulling. The baby just gets…mushed. A lot of them look like coneheads. But that works itself out on its own.

So the final part of the movie scenario is you taking your perfect baby out to meet the family. Forget it. First the baby goes to your wife, who did all the work after all. Then the baby goes to the nurses so he can be weighed and measured and cleaned up. Then there's work to be done on your wife. Then after about an hour, maybe, you get the baby. But if you think they're just going to let you wander around with it, you can forget it. The family can come to the baby, but it's not likely that you'll be carrying the baby to the family.

And bang. That's how fast it happens. You didn't even notice, did you? You are now the third most important person in the family. Out of three!! When it was just you, you were number one. With a bullet, baby! Then you got married and you were like number 1A. But now you're pushed to the side (sometimes literally). And as you watch everyone looking at the baby, and the doctors and family (your wife's – they get dibs) hovering over your wife while you stand in the corner it hits you. Number three. Wow, great. Not exactly a Hallmark moment, huh? But don't worry. This whole book is about how you get back to number one.

A few final thoughts about the pregnancy

As the man, you're sort of dragged through this process without much control over it. But there are some things you can control that I think are critical, and make for a better experience for everyone involved.

Finding Out The Sex – Everyone finds out the sex of the baby. It's fun to know, it makes it easier to pick a name and decorate a nursery, and people who want to give you gifts want to know whether to buy pink or blue. Here's my advice: Don't find out the sex. I didn't. You get very few surprises in this life, but I'm here to tell you that the doctor holding your baby and saying, "It's a..." is unbeatable. I remember that moment with each of my kids, and it is by far one of my best memories of their lives. Of course, I guessed wrong on the sex of all three, so that made it kind of fun, too. Another more practical reason not to find out the sex is it gives you and your wife something to talk about for the entirety of month 9. Believe me, by this time you will have run out of things to say to each other besides, "How much longer until the baby comes?" Being able to talk about whether you're having a boy or a girl is a marriage saver. Plus, later you'll have the fun of telling your son that if he were a girl he would have been named Abigail. And as for those who want you to find out because they want to give you a gift or they're just nosy and want to know, tell them to wait. Or they can buy yellow gifts. Don't underestimate this. Show some backbone and wait to find out.

Natural childbirth – This is a big deal for some people. If it is for you and your wife, then great. Go for it. You probably also run marathons. I ask people who run marathons why they do it and the most popular answer is, "So that I can say that I did it." Well I don't have to run a marathon to say that I did it. I can say that already, so problem solved. It's kind of the same with natural childbirth. I can say I did it without actually going through it. The only thing I will say is this: This decision belongs to your wife. If someone is about to push a pineapple out of your dick, then you can decide whether you'd like some painkillers or you'll just breathe through it. Until then, though, whatever she wants, do that. A friend of mine had her first child naturally. I asked her if it was just exquisitely painful, and she said, "Oh yeah!" Then I asked why she did it, and she said, "Because I'm an idiot." That pretty much summed it up for me.

Cutting the cord – This just stinks of some lame way to get the father involved in the process, and I don't like it. It's stupid. I'm not a surgeon, and I don't like the psychological implications of Daddy physically separating Baby from Mommy. What is that all about? I think it would be WAY cooler if my wife cut her own cord. It would be like cutting your own guts out. Who is going to f**k with a woman who just cut her own guts out. That's a message I'd rather send to the baby any day.

Naming the baby – Please have a name ready for the baby. If your baby is born and you want to get to know him before you name him, just know that I hate you already. And every day that goes by where your parents have to tell their friends that they have a grandchild but don't know what the name is yet, will cause them to start hating you, too. No name is perfect, and it will take you a while to get used to the baby's name. It took about two months with each kid for me to stop saying "the baby" and start using the baby's name. Also, know that your friends can ruin names that you love. For eight months and two weeks we were going to name our daughter Sarah. We loved the name, and had loved it since before we were married. So I mentioned the name to a friend of mine and he said, "I like it. It's kind of Jewish." At the time I thought nothing of it. But over the next two weeks it just ate away at me. "Am I giving my daughter a blatantly Jewish name?" In the end we named her Kate. With our son my mother-in-law actually said, "If it's a boy, choose any name except Luke." So imagine the awkwardness when I introduced her to her grandson, Luke. Another friend was having a boy and started talking names in a restaurant one night. There were about a dozen people there and she said that she was leaning toward the name Sebastian. To that one of her girlfriends said, "You should just name him Kick My Ass Every Day." Everyone at the table howled laughing, and five months later we all met Alexander. Not Sebastian. So beware.

Chapter 2 – The Wrap-Up
1. Pregnancy is about her, not you.
2. Pay attention. Your doctors are not responsible for your wife or this baby. You are.
3. Childbirth is not like it is in the movies. Know your place, don't say anything stupid, and, seriously, don't look.
4. Sebastian? Seriously?

Chapter 3 – THIS MORNING I WAS FRED… NOW I'M… DADDY?

"Well…that was gross."

That's how it goes, too. Yesterday, this morning, two minutes ago – all your life up to this point – you were just Fred. Now you're Daddy.

Boys versus girls

So now you have a baby. After all the puking and

backaches and the nine months that seemed like thirty it's finally here. The first thing you'll notice is that babies come in two kinds – with attachment and without. Before my daughter was born, I knew she would be a boy. I just knew it. A boy was what I wanted, and a boy was what I was getting. Wrong and wrong! I didn't know it at the time, but I really wanted a girl. And if you end up with a girl like I did, don't lose hope.

Girls are great. They talk sooner, sleep better, and go to the emergency room a lot less. Plus they dress cuter. Baby girls have the best clothes and hair. Look at a baby girl sometime and imagine a grown woman wearing her hair and clothes like that. With ruffles across her butt and a tophead ponytail? It's ridiculous. Little girls also have little girl clothes. But little boys dress like little men. Khaki pants, rugby shirt, baseball cap. He'll be dressing the same in college as he did when he was one. Incidentally, I changed my hairstyle when I was thirty-five because I realized that I had had the same hairstyle since my first haircut. I don't know how many grown men are walking around with a haircut that their mother picked out for them, but I know that I am no longer one of them.

If you "got lucky" and had a boy first, take note. Baby girls will make you a better dad. No kidding. With baby girls you'll be all lovey and kissy and tickly and huggy, and that's exactly how you want to be with a little boy. But for some reason we treat our boys differently even though they're only babies. I can't tell you how many little boys I see whose dads call them "buddy" or "pal" and give them high fives instead of kisses. I get it, but here's my advice: treat your baby boy like a baby girl. You would never call your daughter "buddy". Maybe "princess" or "baby" or "sweetheart", but never "buddy" or "pal". Your son can be a "sweetheart", too. He's not your buddy anyway. How many buddies do you have who wear Pull-Ups? And don't be afraid to kiss your son. On the mouth. Now I'm not saying to do this if he's in grad school. But if he's four years old? Smack. Right on the mouth. Don't worry, it doesn't make you gay. He's a baby! Treat him like a baby. Kiss him, hug him, and stop calling him "buddy".

PDSS: Post Delivery Stress Syndrome

After the baby is born you and your wife will be a little drained. Different people handle this in different ways. Just know that your wife had it worse than you did.

I have a friend whose wife had to push for like three or four hours to get their son out. She's tiny – like ninety-five pounds – and that baby did not want to come out. But my friend was a trouper. He stood there next to his wife and coached her and mopped her brow and encouraged her the entire time, and together they got their son into the world. A true team. My friend had racked up some serious new dad brownie points right out of the gate. And then in one move he blew it. Right after the baby was born, while his wife was laying there exhausted, he looked right at her and said, "Man! That was brutal! My feet are killing me!" Way to go, Dad. That comment is now the defining memory of their son's birth. Even if you somehow got stabbed during the delivery, do yourself a favor and keep it to yourself.

Staying in the hospital

After the baby is born the nurses will move you, your wife, and the baby to another room where you'll stay for a couple days. With all three kids this was one of the best times of my life. My wife and I have already decided that we're not having any more kids (at least not with each other), but if we were going to take the leap again, the post-birth hospital stay would factor highly into our decision.

It's hard to explain. Maybe the baby gives off a pheromone or something, but it's like being on the best vacation you ever had. But with gifts. You're relaxed, people stop by to chat and tell you how great you are, and there's nothing on your schedule except what you want to do with your new baby. Your wife is in heaven and has someone besides you to focus on. I can't overstate how much I enjoyed those few days. With the possible exception of...

The baby tests

One thing that I was not prepared for in the hospital was the baby tests. Every once in a while a doctor or nurse will bust in and administer a test on the baby. The two that I remember most vividly were the Heel Blood Test and the Deafness Test.

These weren't the real names of the tests, but they give you an idea of how freaked out I was. In the Heel Blood Test the doctor comes in with a card that has ten circles on it, each about the size of a nickel. Then he punctures your baby's heel with a needle and starts squeezing out the blood like a he's getting the last drops of juice from a lemon. The baby hates this, and she lets everyone know it. Also, ten nickels worth of blood is a lot. And it takes forever to get it out of the baby. I have no idea how long the Heel Blood Test took, but it seemed like five or ten minutes. So I'm standing there watching the doctor squeeze and knead every last ounce of blood out of my one-day old baby while she screams like I've never heard anyone scream before. It's brutal. And here's the kicker: I don't even know what the Heel Blood Test is for. In all three visits to the hospital I was so freaked out that I either forgot to ask or I blocked it and I can't remember.

In the Deafness Test the doctor comes in with a machine and tells you that he's going to determine if your baby can hear. Like right now. No warning, no prep, no pamphlet. In ten seconds he may say, "Your baby is deaf." Man, was I not ready for this one. I was having a good day, I was being a dad, and I was digging the whole new family vibe. And he's going to come in here and tell me that the baby can't hear? Can we make an appointment or something? Seriously, before you can even protest, the test is over. All three of my kids were fine. But I still don't need someone barging into my world and announcing handicaps. There, now you'll know it's coming at least.

Snip snip

If you have a boy there may be one more thing that you have to do before you leave the hospital: the circumcision. I don't know what the conventional wisdom is on circumcision, but I fought against it. I am circumcised (now I bet you're glad you're reading this), but I always wondered what I am missing. I mean, we're still born with foreskin. It's not like it's a tail; we didn't evolve past it. We just choose to cut it off. And I always wondered if guys with foreskin had this great secret that I don't have. Like if you had eleven fingers you could throw a wicked curveball.

So I argued that there was no reason to put my son through this. His manhood should stay intact. My wife countered with a compelling argument. "Hell no. He's getting snipped." Oh. Uh…okay. She explained that she and her friends find uncircumcised penises freaky looking and didn't want anything to do with them. So if I wanted girls to be scared of my son's equipment, then, by all means, skip the snip. So he got snipped.

In retrospect it was a pretty lame argument, but it was good if only because my son knows that he and I are the only boys in the family and he sees that his little mini-pipe looks like Dad's.

So we don't have to have a talk about how I'm hoping that someday he'll be this great Casanova and that's why his junk is different from my junk.

As far as the hospital part of it goes, at least at our hospital they were pretty humane. To me. They took Luke away and brought him back with gauze wrapped around his pee-pee. That wasn't so bad. For me.

Where's the love?

I mentioned that at the beginning of the pregnancy your wife was changing and developing a connection with the baby while you were still your same crass self. So now that the baby is born and you're spending a little time with him, you're thinking that it's your time now. Right? Well it's time for a little honest talk about what happens when your baby is born.

There are all these TV commercials and movie scenes where the new dad is holding his new baby and his eyes are all glassy and he says something stupid like, "It's not just about me anymore." I'm here to tell you that that's a load of B.S.

Now my wife, on the other hand, was weepy at the birth of all three of our kids. But she already had that connection. Besides, I can't be sure that that was love. It could have had something to do with surviving a knockout punch to the groin. No, when the baby is born, it's nice and it's weird, but don't feel bad if you're not blown away like one of those guys on the insurance ads. I wasn't.

My wife's cousin had a baby about three months before we did. Her husband is this great guy. We're totally simpatico. We drink the same drinks, make fun of the same people, and know all the words to the same Judas Priest songs. So before the kids were born we went out and really tore it up. Lots of drinks, lots of "the Priest", and lots of telling everyone we were having kids, which led to lots more drinks.

A few weeks later he had already had his son, so when my

daughter was born I called him up and told him that we had lived through the birth, and then I said something about how big this was. That it changes everything. We weren't the same guys who went out and tore it up a few months ago. There was silence on the other end of the line until he sort of mumbled his agreement, and then we hung up. I have to say, I never felt like such a phony in all my life! I didn't feel like anything had changed. Yeah, we had the baby, but we'd been planning for that. We'd been living with the furniture for months! I remember looking at my daughter and thinking, "I don't even love her. If I had to choose to drop her or my wife off a cliff I'd definitely drop the baby." Don't get me wrong, I love my daughter. And I thought she was pretty neat back then. But she didn't change my life that week, and I didn't love her.

It's okay to admit it. Babies, when they're first born, aren't that cute. I've seen cuter puppies. Plus, newborn babies don't do anything. What's to love there? Now when they get older, fuhgetaboutit. They grow on you fast. And, man, they get cute as a m**********r! They get exponentially cuter. Just when you think they can't possibly get any cuter, BAM, here comes a whole load of new cuteness. In the end I fell hard for all three of my kids, and I would not throw them off a cliff. But if you don't feel the earth move the second you see them, don't sweat it. You just met him or her. There's plenty of time.

So that's what they're for!

I'm going to assume that your wife is breast-feeding the baby. If not, I'm sure you have your reasons. But I think breast-feeding is better than formula, and not because I'm the sensitive, earthy type (you should know me better than that by now). No, I like breast-feeding for reasons that appeal to a man.

First, it's free. Formula costs a ton. But, lucky you, you're sleeping next to a breast milk factory. Second, you can't feed the baby. If the baby gets up in the middle of the night or during the game or when you're on the phone, well goshdarnit you'd like to help out and drop everything and feed her, but you don't have functioning boobs. Eventually your wife will pump milk into bottles and when that's over you'll move to formula, but until then enjoy the free ride.

Going home

The process of leaving the hospital will take about two hours. No kidding. There are forms to sign and just a bunch of delays. So be patient (in case you haven't noticed, that's going to be a theme for you from now on). Also, you'll need to have a baby seat installed in your car. It's possible that the nurse will actually come down and check to see if you're really as much of a moron as she thinks you are and see if there is actually a car seat and if it's installed correctly. But after that you'll get to leave. And make no mistake, they will let you leave with the baby. For some reason that always shocked me.

Depending on which kid this is for you, the actual departure will vary. Our first daughter got into a car that was stuffed with flowers and balloons and was videoed as we drove away. It was like she had just won the NBA championship. Our son got into a car with one bouquet of flowers and his big sister, and we met some people at our house, where he was videoed arriving. Our third child left in a car with her mom and me and didn't even go home. She went straight to Quizno's so we could get lunch for the kids and the in-laws waiting for us at home. Welcome to the world, Baby. Here's Quizno's. Not very Norman Rockwell, is it? You say it won't happen to you, but it will.

The baby at home

Okay, reality-check time. You're a dad now. This book is about how a regular guy (you) becomes a great dad. It starts right here. But like your baby, you'll start with baby steps.

Chapter 3 – The Wrap-Up

1. Whether you had a boy or a girl, treat them the same. They're both babies.
2. Even though the baby is here, remember that it's still all about your wife.
3. Slow down and enjoy the hospital stay.
4. If you don't love the baby yet, don't worry about it. You will soon.

Chapter 4 – YOU AND YOUR BABY AT 0-6 MONTHS

"If you wake the baby I'm going to shoot you in the face."

So you get home with the baby and there's all kind of hullabaloo and visitors (or not). But then it all calms down and eventually it's just you and your wife and the baby. Then it hits you. This is my house, this is my room, that is my TV, but there's a baby here. This baby lives here. Forever. If I don't feed the baby, the baby dies. If I drop the baby, the baby dies. If I breathe wrong, the baby dies. HOW COULD THOSE IDIOTS HAVE LET ME TAKE THE BABY? ?

Your wife is still a wreck and she's tired and hormonal, and you don't know what to do. Well before you call your mommy for help, check this out.

Where are the instructions?

If you can take care of a girlfriend, you can take care of a baby. Notice I said a girlfriend and not a wife. Wives are complicated, girlfriends aren't.

Think back to some of the girls you dated. You probably can't even remember some of them. But if you're honest with yourself, you'll probably see that one of the things that kept you from marrying those girls was that in some way they weren't complicated enough. And I mean that is the best possible way – deep, philosophical, three-dimensional. Complicated. It's a challenge, and we like that. I never get sick of my wife because she's always presenting new facets of herself. She's always a challenge. But girlfriends can be boring. And lucky for you, so can your baby.

If a girlfriend or a baby gets upset, it is manageable because girlfriends and babies have only four basic needs:

1. Feed me.
2. Change me.
3. Burp me.
4. Sleep me.

Feed Me is pretty obvious. Both girlfriends and babies want food. They want you to arrange for it and they want you to pay. If you don't they will cry.

Change Me for babies means get me out of this horrible mess I made into something new and clean before I get a rash. It means pretty much the same for girlfriends except in the case of the girlfriend it will cost you $200 and you won't be solving the problem at CVS.

Burp Me for babies seems obvious, but it can be tricky. Little babies up to about two or three months if I remember correctly, can't burp or fart on their own. You have to kind of bend them over and force it out of them. Girlfriends, however, can burp and fart. But they can still be physically uncomfortable and want you to fix it. Ever run out for some Tylenol in the middle of the night? Ever have to give a massage while you're watching the game? I thought so. Burp Me can also be translated into Hold Me or Comfort Me.

Finally, Sleep Me. I'll talk more about sleep later, but for now just know that babies and girlfriends need to be rested or they get pissed. Babies just need a lot more. Don't let them stay up for more than about two hours at a time. Seriously. With both girlfriends and babies, let them get their rest and you'll have a lot more fun during the time they are awake.

See? You didn't need to call your mom. This is all there is to it. Really. How easy is that, huh? The best news is you already know how to do all this stuff. In fact, you've already done it or you wouldn't have a wife! Just remember, if your baby or girlfriend is fussing, just see to these four needs.

Sweet sweet sleep

At my high school we had senior quotes in the yearbook. It was stupid and unintelligible at the time, but if I look back now it doesn't even seem like English. "Partay, AO! BFRATHSS!! Luv! Remember Tony's? STWQZZ!" Mine was, "Just a homeboy. Be chillin' out. SABOOM!" I think I was trying to say something about our public high school being lily-white, and the "saboom" may have had to do with lighting farts. Obviously I was a deep thinker. But I remember what a friend of mine wrote. It was so great that my friends today, people who have never met this guy, use this quote with me. His quote was, "Sleep is bliss." At the time I thought he was just being weird. But I realize now that he was probably the smartest and most mature person I knew in high school.

You're about to start losing some sleep. But you don't want that to happen to your kids because the more they sleep the happier you will all be. Your children must sleep. It is more important than you know. I recommend that you get a sleep book because you don't know what the hell you're doing. You may think you do, but you don't. It's technical and it's scientific, and you don't know what you're doing. You don't.

In fact, after I had kids I started splitting the world into two groups: those who had read a sleep book and those who hadn't. Just be warned, if you don't read a sleep book and then you go around complaining about or even discussing your kid's sleep patterns, you're going to sound like an idiot and make me hate you. Please don't make me hate you. I want to like you. But I know that most of you will be all like, "What?? Read? I'm already reading! If I wanted to read more I'd go to the can." I know that you think it's boring and pointless and a waste of your free time, but take it from someone who loves watching TV and playing Xbox, you'll be way better off for having read a sleep book.

<u>Healthy Sleep Habits, Happy Child</u> by Dr. Marc Weisbluth worked like a charm for us. Our kids sleep twelve hours a night and took three-hour naps when they were babies. But if you don't like that book, get another one. People protest, saying, "Well, my baby just doesn't want to nap." Yeah, that's neat. And I don't care. Look at it like when you were at camp. There was a rest period sometime during the day. You didn't have to sleep – you could read a book or write a letter – but you had to be in your bunk and be quiet. Until about age 3 or 4 it's the same for naps. Every day. You don't have to sleep, but you have to be in your bed and be quiet.

Let me reiterate, I'm not kidding about the sleep. If you don't get a sleep book or you get one and don't read it, then I hate you. Hell, I have a friend who got a sleep book and then paid someone else nine hundred dollars to explain it to her. Can you believe? But I don't hate her. Hell, have your wife read it and summarize it for you. It'll be like a test of her parenting. She'll love it! But if you get a sleep book, read it, and still don't do what it says because you think you know better than some hoity-toity Ph.D., then you will get everything you deserve and I will laugh at you if we ever meet. Get the point? Sleep is bliss.

You are going to get poop on you

Okay, here we go. You thought that was just a clever title for the book, didn't you? Uh uh. You are going to get poop on you. Say that to yourself.

You're going to get other things on you, too – spit, snot, boogers, vomit, blood. Some of it is even going to go in your mouth. I know, it's chilling, right? But you know what? It's okay. You'll just roll with it. Of course, if you're not a dad already then you can't believe what you're reading. "Holy crap! This Joe Reilly is so disgusting! He's like an animal!! Poop? On me??" Yep. And I'm telling you, you won't care.

When I was in high school I knew this guy who was on the football team. Before practice he would use the facilities in the field house to make his daily constitutional. The stalls, as is the way in every public high school in America, had no doors. So if you walked by this guy while he was in the stall he was known to do this thing that, quite honestly, still seems surreal to talk about today.

When you walked by, especially if you lingered, he would reach down between his legs into the toilet, grab one of his own logs out of the bowl, and throw it at you. Even if it missed, this wet projectile still hit the wall or the floor. It's so horrifying that you almost have to laugh. And it never even happened to me. In fact, I was never in the room when it did happen. But I am still traumatized by even the thought of someone doing something so gross. I mean, OH. MY. GOD. Who does that? Right?? Now that said, I have had to catch poop directly out of the butts of each of my children on more than one occasion. My daughter had one that was perfectly round and hard like a brown lime. When I was changing her it whipped out of the diaper and was headed for the floor. I just reached out and snagged it like I was an All-Star middle infielder. And it didn't bother me at all.

When my son was born, he had an historic discharge. When babies first come out they have this tar-like poop called meconium. They drink the amniotic fluid when they're in the womb and for the first couple of days after they're born they poop tar. It's gross and sticky and Luke had an unlimited amount of it.

I think it was our first night in the hospital with him, and since he was our second kid we were feeling cocky. And then came Luke's meconium. At first it was just regular – he poops, we clean. But the meconium started to form this big bubble, and we didn't know what to do. It was getting bigger and bigger a like black balloon animal. It was like this little tiny baby had the Devil's cucumber floating out of his butt. My wife and I went from staring in amazement to freaking out that this wet poop balloon was going to pop and get meconium everywhere. Finally, we used a diaper and grabbed it and forced it onto the table where the nurse could come get it and take it away. Was I freaked out? Yeah. But was I grossed out? Not at all.

I knew another guy in middle school – in retrospect I didn't go to very good schools – who used to pick his nose and then wipe the boogers on people. He wouldn't just wipe them on your shirt either. He'd wipe them on your arm or your neck or your face! I still get chills when I think about that. But now I'll pick boogers directly out of the noses of my kids. No biggie. I've had vomit in my hair and down my back at the same time. Because being a dad is dirty business. And it all starts with you getting pooped on. That's the foundation.

That's important: the foundation. Like anything that you're building, the foundation is the key. It starts early – like right now. My oldest is eleven, so she's past the foundation-building years, but she has a good one. I don't worry too much about her being a teenager because I know she has that good foundation. Of course, since I don't have a teenager I don't know what I'm talking about there. So who knows? There may be a book out there in about eight years with my name on it entitled <u>How to Kill Your Teenager and Get Away With It</u>.

But for now I have a theory that the foundation is laid and love is earned between the ages of 0 and 5. In other words, by the time your kid is five you have laid the groundwork on which you're going to build for the rest of his life. So don't neglect it. Also, by this time they will have earned a lifetime's worth of love from you. So when they're fourteen and wreck your car you'll look at their baby pictures and remember how much you loved them, and they'll benefit from that now. After age five, though, they stop listening. And they start to lose their cuteness anyway. By the time they're fourteen, they're hideous and they're ashamed of you. God help them if they haven't earned your love by then. If they don't have a good foundation by then? Then you should just move.

The battle ahead

So now you know some stuff. Hell, you know more than 95% of new dads know. But don't get cocky. The British got cocky. Napoleon got cocky. Remember what they have in common? Even with your new knowledge, you have not yet won the battle. Because make no mistake, that's what is coming – a battle.

When your baby is between zero- and three-months old, you're in combat mode. You eat, sleep, shop, bathe, breathe, and work when the enemy allows you to. When the enemy brings the fight to you, you are always ready. Day or night. Rain or shine. You will not be defeated because you are as relentless as your enemy. You will remain vigilant and adopt battle tactics. There's a saying in British Special Forces: weapon, kit, self. In other words, when there's a lull in the action, you ready your weapon, then your equipment, then yourself. That way if the enemy attacks again, you are ready to fight.

I'm sorry to say that your cute little Freddy Junior is the enemy. In those first few months he will come at you day and night. Sometimes he'll sleep for hours, other times for only minutes. He'll poop, you'll change him, and he'll immediately poop again. He'll eat and not be able to burp. Then when he does burp, he'll barf all over the clothes that you just put him in. He'll want to play, not realizing that it's four in the morning. It's nothing short of a battle. But if you stay vigilant and PREPARED, you can win the battle. Just remember: weapon, kit, self.

If Freddy Junior is sleeping or quiet, get your weapons in order. This is anything related to Feed Me, Sleep Me, Burp Me, and Change Me. Diapers, wipes, food, clothes, burp cloths, etc. Then get your kit in order. This is anything that helps you battle him. Clean clothes, toys where they are reachable, clean spare bottles, food ready, find the pacifier, etc. Finally, self. Get yourself in order. Eat, bathe, change clothes, make phone calls, and sleep.

It's hard to believe that this will go on for a couple of months, but it does. You'll live – it's not exactly storming the beach at Normandy. And you'll win this battle – mainly because you're an adult and Freddy will outgrow this stage. Then, like with most traumatic things, you'll forget. Sometime in the future you and your wife will contemplate having another baby and you won't even remember pushing the stroller around your apartment at three in the morning in your boxers. You'll just smile and try to remember and say, "Yeah, that was hard." But you won't have any real remembrance of it. Which is the only reason you'll agree to have another baby.

Of course, this all assumes that you have a baby that doesn't have colic. If that happens (and colic happens about 20% of the time), you are well and truly F****D. Colic is not your run-of-the-mill enemy. Colic is the Red Army, the Viet Cong, and all of those dudes from Braveheart rolled into one. You will just hope that you survive and you will remember every minute of it, and I pity you. But the mantra remains the same: weapon, kit, self.

The Magic Bullet

But even though they are your enemy, all babies have a Magic Bullet – even colicky ones. And it's a biggee. No matter who you are it will cause you to love them more than pizza after ten beers at four a.m. It's the reason why people always want you to see their babies and why dogs can't compete with babies for your love. What is the Magic Bullet you ask? Just two ingredients.

Babies are one-half the person you find so attractive that you agreed to spend the rest of your life with only them. When you saw them you felt weak and you had to announce to the world that they were your soulmate. And that's the weaker half of the Magic Bullet. The other half of your baby, the potent half, is the person you find most attractive, charming, and magnetic in the whole world. More than your wife, more than your mother, more than Angelina Jolie and Scarlett Johannson combined – it's you.

Is that a wicked combination or what? Is it any wonder people think their own babies are so cute? And babies don't really even get cute until about three months old. But that didn't stop us! In our apartment we have so many huge framed pictures and mouse pads and t-shirts and mugs and art with our daughter's picture before she was three months old on them that it's embarrassing. I look at some of that stuff now (because how could we possibly have thrown any of it away?) and wonder what we were thinking. She wasn't cute at all. She was kind of ugly. And a little mutant looking. It's embarrassing. But, man, we were under the spell. Along about three months old, though, your baby will start to get legitimately cute and deploy his Magic Bullet. At that point the battle will be forgotten. But until then, dig in.

Never say never

The Magic Bullet is so potent, in fact, that it will cause you to completely reverse yourself on statements you've made publicly. Before I was a dad, and especially when I was single, I would make these grand pronouncements. "I'm not getting married before I have one million dollars in the bank!" (As it turned out, I missed that mark by only about… a million dollars). Or, "I would never put anything as harmful as drugs into my body!" (Which I never have, but I was very very drunk when I said that). Even if I was wrong – which as you can see, I was – I would never admit it.

Well, that behavior carried over after I had kids. Specifically, I remember the following:

"I will never indulge my kids by cutting the crusts off of their sandwiches."

"I will never pay more for commercial items just because they have my kids' favorite characters on them."

"My kids will never play video games in a restaurant. That is family time."

Well, I'm here to tell you that I admit it. I was wrong. My kids are no crust eating, Dora the Explorer lunchbox having, video game playing proof for all my friends to see that you should never say never. You'll be surprised what you'll do for your kids.

Going back to work

Whether you or your wife or both have a job that you need to get back to, it's okay. There's this thing with new parents (mostly moms) where they think that they have to be home with the baby or the baby will miss out on some vital element that will then cause him to get into the wrong preschool which will lead to the wrong grade school, high school, and college, at which point he will have a bad life. All this because you selfishly went back to work. Don't worry about it, especially at this stage. All you are missing is about five hours of awake time and a few diapers. Besides, you want to go back to work to set the tone for later. In a year or two this baby is going to start acting like a total pain in the ass and a little quiet time at the office is going to start looking pretty good, believe me.

This is going to sound stupid, but…

…Don't forget the baby. This is especially important for us men. Women already think we don't know what we're doing. So if you get careless with the baby early on you'll never get that trust back.

I know that you're thinking that this is a no-brainer, but it's not. You've been running around your whole life with just you to worry about. Even when you took on a wife she was still an adult, and if you left her behind she was responsible for finding her own way home. But you have to remember that the baby is there. She's little and she's quiet and she doesn't know that you just left her in the men's room. I know, I hear you, "Joe, come on, a little respect. Please. I'm not gonna forget the baby." Oh yeah? Have you ever been at a restaurant and had the rest of your food boxed up to take with you and then gotten home and realized that you left the food sitting on the table? Yeah, that's what I thought.

One time I was picking up my daughter from preschool. I parked, went in, signed her out, and we left. Then we decided that since it was a nice day we would walk up the street with some of her classmates to the ice cream store. So we went, had ice cream, and chit-chatted with the other parents until it was time to go home. So Kate and I walked back to the car and I looked in the back window and there was my four-month old son staring back at us. Holy crap, I totally forgot about Luke! I was thinking about Kate and I wasn't used to Luke yet and I left him in the car for about an hour. An hour! Thank god we were in cool California and not broiling Texas and he was sitting in a very comfortable sixty-five degree car. He didn't even care. He was just hanging out. But I cared. And a week later when I told my wife what happened, she really cared. I think that that's a nightmare that women have: that their idiot husband is going to walk off without the baby. That they'll just come home one day and say, "Hi, Honey."

"Hi. Where's the baby?"
"Uh… I'll be right back."
Don't be that guy.

Wham bam thank you ma'am

At some point your wife will allow you to have sex with her again. It won't be pleasant. But be aware, whether your wife is having her period or not, whether she just had the baby a few weeks ago, she can get pregnant again. Let me say that again: she can get pregnant again right now. It happens, it has happened, and it will happen again. You, New Dad, are not ready for another baby. So take whatever precautions you take to not make babies. You'll be ready for a new baby someday, but you're not ready now.

Rover and the baby

A quick note here if you have a dog. People with dogs think that their dogs are adorable. Occasionally they are right. If you have a dog, you may be inclined to say the following:

- The baby will never replace my dog. I LOVE my dog.
- I have a special relationship with my dog.
- I don't know if I'll love the baby more than my dog.
- I will always think my dog is cuter than the baby.
- Nothing will change the way I feel about my dog.

If you find that you have even thought such foolishness, go find a big book of baby pictures and smack yourself over the head with it. And if you've already said any of these things to people you'll ever see again, start preparing your retraction.

I have a friend who has two pugs, and he swore all of the above statements to me. He loves his dogs so much that if there were some sort of civil commitment ceremony where you could express to the world your love for your dogs, then he'd be the first in line. But then he had a baby. Then the baby smiled at him. Game, set, match – baby. I haven't seen those pugs in four years. Even he admitted that the baby, being human and all, was cuter than the dogs.

Love your dogs. Just remember that they don't have the Magic Bullet, so they don't stand a chance.

So there's Chapter 4. The baby is now six-months old and you know a lot of stuff. But now that you know all this, most of you still will have one significant problem. The baby is becoming a kid. And you're wondering, How in the hell do I take care of a kid? But don't worry. You already know how to take care of a kid. You just don't know you know.

Chapter 4 – The Wrap-Up
1. Feed me, change me, burp me, sleep me.
2. Get a sleep book and read it. Don't make me hate you.
3. You are going to get poop on you. It's more than just a title!
4. Never say never. The Magic Bullet is ridiculously powerful.
5. Humans > Dogs.

Chapter 5 – RAISING A KID
YOUR BABY AT 6-24 MONTHS

"Let's say, hypothetically, that a baby got on the elevator. What floor do you think he would get off on?"

One of the great things about kids is that they ease you into taking care of them. A lot of dads see other dads with older kids and the dads look like they are in such a groove. They just have the whole dad rhythm down, and it makes new dads nervous.

A friend of mine was about to have a baby and he called me with a list of questions. Soon I could tell that the questions were all based on his nervousness about his lack of experience being a dad. Like he wanted to know how we came up with the word "dupa". A "dupa" is a butt. My wife had a friend who has Slavic ancestry and she said that "dupa" was Slavic for butt. I don't know if that's actually true or not, but it stuck. So we (and the kids) started calling our butts "dupas" or "dupes" for short. My friend wanted to know about that, and he was getting a little panicky about the whole process in general. What he didn't understand was that he didn't need to worry about that kind of stuff yet. Because your kids will ease you into parenting.

Newborns do nothing. Literally. You can put them on a ledge and they can't roll off*. This is good because (1) ledges are dangerous and (2) nothing is about all we can handle. But by the time the baby gets to six months old, we're starting to feel pretty good about ourselves and we're ready for some new challenges. But even still, the baby knows to go slow.

*The baby mentioned here is imaginary. Your baby is real. Do not put your real newborn on a ledge.

Sitting

I know, woo woo woo, sitting. How exciting. But one day you're going to put Freddy Jr. down and he's not going to fall over like a sack of dog food. He's just going to sit there, ramrod straight. And you're going to be thrilled. You're going to clap your hands together like an old lady and say, "Yea, Freddy!" You're gonna video it. You just wait.

Crawling

The next thing Freddy is going to do is crawl. By the way, these milestones happen when the kid is ready, not when you are or when your sister's kid did them. My daughter spoke Spanish at fifteen months, but didn't walk until about the same time. My son walked at seven months, but didn't speak English until he was two and a half. So give your kids a break.

So when Freddy crawls, he's suddenly mobile. He can leave the room. He can leave the house. So you see what he's doing? He's helping you out. He knows that you're a rookie, so he's saying, "Okay, Dad, you have to keep an eye on me now. But soon I'll be able to walk and then run. Then you'll have to never take your eyes off me. But for now just practice keeping an eye on me."

So he cruises around and you keep an eye on him while at the same time becoming a more capable, experienced dad. You're both learning to crawl.

Pulling Up

Once you get used to crawling, Freddy will pull up on things. It's not standing yet because he can't hold himself up or balance, but it's close. Pulling up doesn't add any more difficulty in terms of mobility, but what Freddy has done is add the third dimension.

Before, you only had to be concerned about the width and depth of the room, i.e. the floor. But now Freddy had added height. Now he can reach your glass on the coffee table. He can reach the scissors, your briefcase, the remote control, and the dog's tail. He can also reach the detergent tray in an open dishwasher.

This happened to me when I was one-year old. I pulled up on the dishwasher, dipped my fingers in the detergent tray, and choked on some Cascade. I was rushed to the emergency room with burns in my tiny esophagus and the doctors weren't sure if I was ever going to be able to speak. I ended up okay. I can speak and I don't sound like Alec Baldwin or anything. I can even yell. Loudly. But it's a good lesson. Once the baby adds the dimension of height it is time for you to start paying closer attention.

Walking

If Freddy Jr. has done his job, then by now you're pretty well trained. In fact, you'll be eager for him to walk. The only trick is that he will probably walk before he can talk, making it difficult for you to communicate things like, "Don't run in the street," or "Come here," or "Where are you?" Also, soon after walking comes running. As in Away From You. But by this point you will have a pretty good read on Freddy and his schemes. He's taken over a year to get to this point and he's brought you along slowly. Now, believe it or not, newer dads are watching you and feeling nervous. They're wondering if they can be as on top of it as you are. I know, hard to believe.

Cause and effect

In this age period it's going to be difficult to teach your kid any lessons because he doesn't understand cause and effect. I had to learn this one the hard way. No matter how many times you tell them that if they touch the stove they will get burned, kids this age can't make that connection. In fact, if your daughter is like mine, she will touch the stove, look surprised, tell you that it is hot, and then touch it again. So don't waste your breath on rules or discipline. There will be plenty of time for that later. For now, just know that when you tell them that if they play with Daddy's stuff Daddy will be mad, all they are hearing is, "Blah blah blah Daddy blah blah blah blah Daddy."

However, even though they are not making that causal connection, your kids will still react to things – like touching a hot stove. So here's a little trick to make this time easier: Your kids will react to things the same way you react to things.

Here's how it works. If Junior runs into the door and bonks his nose, he will look to you before reacting. If you have older kids, you've seen this. Junior is looking at you and thinking, "Wow, doors are hard and noses are soft. That sucked." But this is new to him, so he doesn't know what to make of it. So he looks at you.

If you rush over and freak out and start with, "Omigod, omigod, omigod! Are you okay??" Junior will see your panic and he will know that this is a big deal. He'll know that this is how he should react, too, and he will cry. But if you take a different approach to the nose slamming by saying, "Bonk!" and then you laugh, he'll see that and he'll laugh, too. It's like a magic trick.

I know that it sounds weird, but I'm telling you that it works. It may even feel weird at first as your kid falls out of his chair and hammers into the ground face first and you plaster a smile on your face and go, "Whoopsie!" But it works. Of course, if they're really hurt, they won't look to you; they'll cry instantly. But what you've given them by doing this is a way to shake off the little stuff. It's like an intermediate emotion, which is a good thing to have. My kids still use it today.

Chapter 5 – The Wrap-Up
1. Don't panic. Your kid is moving as slowly as you are.
2. React to things the way you want your child to react to things.

Chapter 6 – THEY'RE NOT BABIES ANYMORE
YOUR CHILD AT 2-3 YEARS

"Do not make me set down this beer."

Okay, here we go. This is what you've been reading all this time for. Here is where we officially get down to business. It is during this age range that you will set yourself up to either be a great dad or just a good one. In other words, we've now gotten to the point I like to call…

THE MEAT OF THE BOOK

Let me start by saying that once you've been suckered into reading this whole book, your friends don't have to. What you'll do is you'll give them a copy of the book, but tell them to skip to here. It's easy because they can look for that big MEAT OF THE BOOK sign. You'll get tons of credit with the wives, including yours, for being so thoughtful, and your friends won't hate you for giving them an extra chore. It's a win-win. Besides, this part right here is the only reason I wrote the book anyway. All the stuff before this is nice, but I think it is stuff that you could learn on the fly. However, you may not get anything more valuable out of this book than what comes next – except for the credit of appearing to be a modern, caring dad. We know that you're not that, but we can fake it and keep it to ourselves. So get ready…

The Meat of the Book – Part 1
R-E-S-P-E-C-T

In one way or another all the relationships in your life are based on and revolve around one thing – Respect. The popular wisdom here is that the answer is love. But that's wrong. Love is easy. You love your dog, you love your car, you love Cuban cigars. But do you respect any of them? And don't tell me that you respect your dog. He licks his own butt. End of story. Respect is hard. It's hard to give and it's hard to earn. But that's exactly how it works. It goes both ways like that. You have to have that with your kids. Have to. And it works for marriages, too.

Joestradamous

I have the ability to look at a couple and tell if they're going to make it. I can almost always predict when a relationship will end in divorce. It used to be that people thought I was some sort of ghoul, just predicting marriage breakups. Until I was right.

Then they thought I was just guessing. I mean, the divorce rate is fifty percent. But my average was way higher than that. More like ninety-five percent. Then they just started to flat out ask me, "So, Joe, we've been together two years. We're thinking about getting married. What do you think?" Well, uh...

One time I was at a wedding and my wife's aunt asked me about her daughter and her daughter's boyfriend. They're perfect together, right? They're going to get married, aren't they? I know that she asked me just to validate her feeling that this was a good relationship, and it was a fun environment with lots of family and friends around. But I had been drinking and I've never been one to hold my tongue, so I looked at this perfect couple and declared, at this blessed family event, that they had no hope. This was met with silence and then laughter. Oh, Joe's just kidding. But because I'm an ass and was committed to ruining everyone's weekend, I insisted. No no, they are doomed.

Well, the word spread like wildfire. There was no one at this wedding who hadn't heard what I had said, and the reactions were a mixture of fascination and loathing. It was like I was a giant spider. Of course, my wife's aunt and uncle thought I was a jackass, and I couldn't really disagree. I should have just kept my mouth shut. Or better yet, lied! But what I saw in that couple was so obvious to me. He did not respect her. That was it. They would never spend a lifetime together because he didn't respect her. He may have loved her, but he didn't respect her. There is a difference. Within a few months they were broken up. He married another girl shortly thereafter. She has since married another guy (they're going to last, by the way).

I don't have a lot of helpful anecdotes about my family because, quite honestly, they suck. But this is one that's worth mentioning. My sister is divorced, and I can sum up the problem with her marriage in three words: the middle seat. My former brother-in-law is a big guy – like 6-foot-three and broad shouldered. He's bigger than any of the men in my family. One time we were on a family trip and we were returning from Europe. It was going to be a long flight, like ten or fourteen hours. When my sister got on the plane, she took the window seat in a row where the aisle was already taken, leaving the middle seat for her husband. He asked her if she wouldn't mind switching, but she refused, stating that it was her turn to sit in the window. So I watched as my brother-in-law wedged his broad shoulders and long legs into the middle seat for a ten-hour-plus plane ride. I remember thinking right then, "Wow, my sister doesn't respect her husband. They're never going to make it." And even though he married her, bought her cars and a house and had three kids with her, he eventually left. He said she made him feel lousy. It came down to respect.

That's how much it matters. You have to, have to, HAVE TO have it in the relationships in your life. Your kid is one of your biggest relationships. So how do you get respect?

Getting respect

Have you ever had anyone say that you had to respect him? Or listen to him? Or do anything regarding him? That you HAD to? How did you feel about that person? Did you want to respect him or listen to him? Or did you want to bash his head in with a frying pan (maybe that's just me)?

With anyone, but with your kids especially, the key to getting respect is to give it. That's right, give it. I know that your kid is two- or three-years old, and she's still a baby to you. But at this age she has needs and wants and opinions. Respect them.

Of course, you want to do so within the framework of safety, but outside of that feel free to hear out her thoughts and feelings. Here's a good rule of thumb: In general, treat your kids as if they are older than they are. Don't you wish someone had done that for you? Or would even today? Don't you wish someone would have said to you, "Okay, if that's what you want to do, go ahead." Even if you totally botched whatever it was you wanted to do, what would have you learned? For one, you would have learned the way not to do it. But even better, you would have learned that the object of your respect (e.g. your parents) trusts you and respects your decision-making ability.

Now if your son decides that he wants to play with razor blades, you have to step in. It is unsafe. But if he wants to help put the cake in the oven? Yeah, he might drop it. Or he might burn himself. But he probably won't, and this is a chance for you to show that you respect him enough to let him handle something that you've worked on.

Your child is an inexperienced little person. Respect him for that alone. He doesn't know a damn thing, but he's trying. And he's going to make a lot of mistakes. A lot. But one of the beauties of respecting your children is that when they act up, you can address it from that place rather than just being a boss telling them what to do.

For example, if Freddy throws his dinner on the floor, don't just say, "Don't do that." That's bossing. Besides, you're creating conflict. You know he wants to do it. He already did it. Now you're taking a contrary position. Instead, ask him, "When you make something for me, do I throw it on the ground?" See the difference?

Freddy understands that you respect the things that he makes and he wants you to continue to do so. If you were to suddenly start crumpling his art up and throwing it on the ground, he would be hurt. Now he can understand how you feel when he throws his dinner on the floor. You're saying to him, "I respect you, please respect me." The other way you're just bossing, and no one likes to be bossed.

It works for older kids and bigger problems as well. If a child steals from you, that is disrespectful. You would never go into their room or car or wallet and take their stuff without asking. So since we're not bossing, the question here is, "By stealing, are you telling me that you want me to steal from you?" The implication from you is that that is where you are headed. You can each buy a safe to keep your valuables in, and then you can both keep watch on your stuff day and night. "Because if you're going to steal from me (disrespect me), then I'm going to steal from you (I disrespect you) whatever I can whenever I can. The alternative is we respect each other and each other's property. But because I respect you, I'll let you choose what we should do." And then you let him choose. A note, however: Kids are stubborn – be prepared to buy a safe and fill it with Ipods, jewelry, shoes, toothbrushes, etc. while pulling spending money from their piggy banks until they get the point.

Also, if the problems become all about your kid and don't involve you – like drugs or cutting – then you're now talking about self-respect. Luckily, these problems won't arise until later and you will have had time to teach your child about respect in general. Then, when the time comes, you can refocus the discussion on self-respect.

But it sounds too hard

I'll admit, even as I'm writing this I'm thinking, "This is too much to tackle. Even I'm getting intimidated." But it's not too hard. It's certainly not any harder than learning to walk, talk, eat, use the toilet, use a fork, or any number of things your kid is learning. And you already did all those things. Just keep it simple. Always. Keep bringing it back to, "I don't do that to you, so please don't do it to me."

A trick you can use early on to show your kids your respect for their decisions is to give choices. For example, "Do you want to brush your teeth or take a bath?" The choices are set up so that there really is no choice. Either way, your child is doing what you want him to do. But what you're giving him is the illusion of choice. You're not bossing. You're showing respect for him as a human being by asking what he wants to do. This works as your kids get older, too. You just have to be cleverer with it. "Don't forget, you still have piano and homework to do," is bossy and generates an irritated response. But "Do you want to do your piano or your homework first?" is more respectful, and your kids will notice the difference.

Of course, you won't be perfect. You'll do it wrong or say it wrong, and sometimes you will just lose it. You'll say exactly the wrong thing in public and way too loud. But that's okay. First, it's okay because we're not parenting geniuses, right? Damn right! We're not trying to be. Remember that. We're doing the best we can and picking up some useful tools along the way. Second, it's okay to lose it every once in a while. People have this aversion to raising their voices at their kids. I don't have that aversion. Kids respond to that if it's used in the right places. Imagine if someone eighteen feet tall yelled at you. But I like it because it carries an implied threat. You're saying, "Please respect me", but you're implying, "Or else." It's effective and you shouldn't be embarrassed to use it.

But most of the time, if you're looking to give respect to your kids, they'll know it. More times than not you'll come from the right place and say the right thing. Or close enough to it. And they'll sense that.

Do I know enough now?

My answer is going to surprise you. Yes, you know what you need to know. I told you that that was the meat of the book, and I wasn't kidding. Just remember, "Respect is not love; give and get respect," and you can stop reading. Of course, you'll miss the companion piece to Respect, plus all the great stuff and funny stories that I've been saving for those of you who aren't quitters. C'mon, these are your kids. Don't be such a baby!

A final word on respect

You will love your kids. Even when they are a pain in the ass. That's the easy part. You will love them and they will love you. They have the Magic Bullet, remember? But if your kids respect you and who you are, and you give it back, you've got 'em. The battle is won. They will have a rock-solid foundation for you to build on. And I know some of you are thinking, "What a bunch of crap! Blah, blah, blah. Hey, Joe, respect this!" Okay. But think of the people in your life who you respect. Your dad, your boss, Derek Jeter. Whoever it is, how do you feel if they respect you? Good, right? That's right. So suck on that!

Just beware, one sure way to not get respect is to use the word Respect. As in, "You will respect your mother!" It just doesn't work. Respect happens through action. You don't need to mention it. Feel free to mention love all the time. Say it, talk about it, use it. Love love love. See, isn't that nice? But don't mention respect.

When my son, Luke, was two he couldn't really talk yet, and it was really frustrating to him. Especially when he really had something to say, like, "Hey dumbass, I was using that ball!" So since he couldn't talk, he screamed. And when I say screamed I mean this ear-splitting, glass-shattering, spine-bending shriek that would cause people outside to wonder what we were doing in the house. It was really embarrassing because (a) it was super loud and (b) it was really girly. Like super girly. But what could we do? So my wife and I decided (with the help of Luke's preschool teacher, whose idea it was) to give him respect. When he got worked up like that, we would give him the words, "Wow, Luke, you're feeling really mad, aren't you?" Or, "It upset you when your sister sat in your chair." It totally worked. The screaming stopped because we showed Luke that we get it and we respect his feelings. Just saying, "Stop screaming," would not have worked. He was two-years old and the respect thing worked. Just try it.

Chapter 6 – The Wrap-Up

1. Respect > Love.
2. Give respect to get it.
3. Treat your kids as if they were older than they are.
4. "I don't do that to you, so please don't do that to me."
5. No bossing.

Chapter 7 – YOU'RE A BIG KID NOW, AND SO ARE THEY
YOUR CHILD AT 3-5 YEARS

"Remember, Son, wear your backpack, listen to your teachers, and don't eat your friends."

Remember earlier when I said that your kids don't understand cause and effect so you can't discipline them? Well now they do and you can. We've talked about Respect; now we're going to talk about your other weapon – Discipline.

The Meat of the Book – Part 2
Discipline

Now that we have respect going back and forth, and there's some order in the family, what's next? What's next is Discipline.

I love love love discipline. And I'm not talking about spanking, which is a common misconception in this country. Spanking is punishment. We say we are "disciplining" someone, but what we're really doing is punishing him. It's a misnomer that has found its way into our lexicon. No, discipline comes from within. It is control. It is what gets people out of bed for work in the morning, keeps a cornerback from biting on a hook and go, and allows you to laugh at your boss's joke instead of setting him on fire. You want your kids to have discipline.

"Well, duh! Of course, I want them to have discipline." Fair enough. But it's more important than you know. When your kids are young they'll need discipline to counter their overwhelming urge to kill themselves just to see if they can. Remember me with the dishwasher soap? Later, they'll need it to achieve at anything. And along the way, both of you will need it to keep your relationship going in the right direction.

No bossing

Yeah, I know, I said "relationship" before. Most of us don't think of our kids as people we have a "relationship" with. I certainly don't. I think it's because it suggests an even playing field that doesn't exist early on. But it happens soon. And the sooner you can get there, the better off you'll be in the eyes of your kid.

Discipline is tied to respect. From respect comes discipline and from discipline comes more respect. Once you have discipline, you don't need rules. We touched on bossing before, but it's worth mentioning that people who boss other people don't respect them. And the bossie always knows it. Have you ever gone over to someone else's house and done something – worn your shoes inside, wandered around with a glass of water, moved a chair into a more convenient spot – only to be told that it was against the rules? "Oh. Yeah. We only drink drinks in the kitchen. It's a rule." I cannot tell you how much I hate b******t like that. Houses like that usually have pages of rules containing all the things you can't do in, around, or to the house. The reason that certain households have so many rules is that they are lacking in respect or discipline.

In your house, you want to have discipline. You don't want to have a bunch of rules. First off, you have to think of them all. Then you have to post them. Then you have to enforce them. And every rule has a different punishment for breaking it. What's the punishment for drawing on the wall? How about giving Tylenol to the dog? What do you get for emptying a bag of flour in your sister's bed? See? It's a total pain. No, you want discipline, not rules. You want your family to run like a SEAL team.

Seal Team Smith

Remember in the introduction when I said that I was fascinated by the Navy SEALs? Well I am. SEAL teams are totally efficient. They're all about the integrity of the unit and getting the job done. If one team member is lagging, the others pick up the slack. They all know what their assignments are, they all do them, and then they all go home. No job goes undone and no one gets left behind. Now let me ask you a question: Do you think that SEAL teams boss each other around? Do you think that they have a bunch of rules?

- Always put your name on your parachute.
- Don't share flippers.
- Always shoot your enemy in the face.

No, of course not. What they do have is respect – for each other, for the unit, for the job – and discipline. The functionality of the unit is so important that they would never act in a way that would require a rule. Discipline trumps that. If you can get your family to operate with that kind of efficiency, I promise that you will never have another kid-related problem again.

But, of course, kids are not Navy SEALs. Hell, most men are not Navy SEALs. I understand that Navy SEALs are highly trained special operators, and Freddy Jr. is only four and still making boom-booms in his Pull-Ups. But what's important is that you establish a culture for Freddy that shows him that the functioning of the family unit is important. To everyone. Including him.

When Freddy thinks about taking a hammer to your new plasma TV, you want him to think about what he's doing and how he's disrupting the family dynamic. Now this is a sophisticated thought process for someone about to hit a TV with a hammer, but it comes in steps over time. Step one is just to get Freddy to stop. And the way to do that is to count one, two, three.

I know, you're thinking, "One, two, three? Seriously? Gee, thanks, Joe. Guess I can skip ahead here!" But wait, there's more. I realize that most parents give their kids the ol', "I'm going to count to three. One… Two… etc." But I also realize that they leave off the best part - which goes like this: *"And then I'm going to help you do it."* Bam! Isn't that great? I learned that from my kids' preschool and I'm telling you that it's gold.

Kids, especially when they are little, love to do things for themselves (and hate for you to do things for them). So when you say, "On the count of three, either you do it or I'm going to help you do it," they realize what's happening. Either way, Daddy is getting what he wants. Then that Little Kid defiance kicks in and they react by depriving you of the pleasure of helping them and do it themselves. Sure, they're surly and giving you the evil eye, but who cares? They're doing what you want them to do!

Don't underestimate that phrase. "And then I'm going to help you do it." It will last you a long long time. Eventually, though, as Freddy matures, he needs to know on his own that when that hammer hits that TV he has crossed the line. He has strayed from the culture of the family because we don't behave that way (because of... that's right, respect - I don't do that to your stuff, please don't do it to mine, remember?) And he knows that there will be consequences because everyone, not just Mom and Dad, put the smooth operation of the family first. Wouldn't that be great?

The flipside is that you have a rule that says, "We don't hit the TV with a hammer." The consequences for breaking that rule may be punishment, but the rule still appears arbitrary. Especially to a four year old. Believe me, as a former kid who may or may not have hit the TV with a hammer, if I got punished for breaking the rule "We don't hit the TV", the very next thing I would do is hit the radio. Or the toaster. Or the car. Or my brother. No one ever said anything about hitting those things! That would be called lack of discipline and lack of respect – a problem that Navy SEALs don't have.

You're in the Army now

The Navy SEALs are a goal to aspire to, but not achieve.

You can start Freddy Jr. out as a Private. Army, Navy, Air Force, Marines, Coast Guard, National Guard; I like the military in general in terms of discipline. A lot of people complain to me about something that their kid does or won't stop doing, and I often think that their kid could use a week in the Army.

The Army demands discipline. What would happen to Freddy Jr. if he were in the Army and wouldn't stay in bed? Easy, the Army would rain thunder down on Freddy until he got the message. The military is totally inflexible on stuff like that. If you disobey, punishment comes hard and fast. If you continue to disobey, the punishment ratchets up exponentially. In the Army if you disobey enough, you can go to jail!

When they say to do something, they expect you to do it, and you had better do it right now. Your kids need the same from you. You need to command their respect, and then you'll reciprocate it. Look at it this way: the military puts everyone through Basic Training, but then it turns around and gives them guns and planes and ships and bombs. Respect is given and respect is received.

Sergeant Dad? I don't think so

Of course, you don't have jail as a recourse (unless your kid is really going to jail, in which case I apologize for being so lazy and not writing this book ten years ago when you needed it.) And you may be worried about what punishments are appropriate. Or whether you can dish them out.

Again, I would defer to the Navy SEALs. First, even some SEAL instructors can't be the "bad cop". They just don't have it in them. I do. I love being the "bad cop". But if you don't maybe your wife does. If both of you are just too nice and decent, just take this in and do the best you can.

SEAL instructors seem to invent punishments that are painful for the offenders, but amusing to them. They have trainees get wet and roll in the sand until they look like sugar cookies. They have them swim in mudholes or even hang upside down from an obstacle. I like this approach a lot. It keeps things interesting and keeps people on their toes.

If your kid throws a ball in the house, why not make him clean his room using only his feet? If he talks back, make him count backwards from 100. If he leaves his shoes outside, make him do 20 push-ups. I'm just making this stuff up, but the point is you're punishing him and it's not a big pain for you. Also, he'll know what is happening. Freddy messed up, so Daddy gets to have some fun at his expense. It gets the message across without it being the end of the world. You're telling him, "We both know that you messed up. I don't hold it against you. Just pay the price and we'll move on. No biggie." There's a level of respect there that doesn't exist with ordinary scowling punishment. Who knows, maybe he'll even have fun. It will certainly make you a more interesting parent. And before you start with the whole, "I don't know, Joe. This just seems weird," let me remind you that we were spanked. At least I was. So I don't see how having to wear shoes and socks on your hands for an hour is any worse than that.

Boys versus girls, part 2

We talked earlier about treating boys and girls the same when they are kids – mostly when it comes to showing affection. But as they get older you will need to treat them differently, especially when it comes to punishment.

Boys and girls are just wired differently. The way they play, the intensity of their physical contact, and their emotional reactions vary widely. From the time my son could manipulate things with his little hands, he was making things into guns. We don't own any guns, and it's not like I'm watching Rambo with him. He just knew what guns were and wanted to shoot stuff. When he was about two years old he turned a piece of toast into a gun. Toast. Neither of my daughters has ever acted this way.

I remember one time Luke was about four years old and he was sitting next to me on the couch and we were playing a game. He was using his near hand and trying to slap my face (again, not a game my daughters are interested in), and I was doing "wax on" and "wax off" to block him. After a few tries to smack me followed by a few successful blocks by me, Luke reached all the way across with his far hand and punched me in the mouth. Hard. I couldn't believe it. I was stunned. I never saw it coming, but my Karate Kid moves wouldn't have helped anyway.

I didn't punish him if that's what you're thinking. Actually I was tickled that he saw such an obvious opening and took advantage of it. But I bring this up to point out that boys and girls play and react to play differently. Discipline that works for one may not work for the other. A punishment that works for one may be totally ineffective on another. You have to stay creative, remember to respect them as individuals, and treat them that way.

Now is that it?

To quote a friend of mine who, when asked if he liked a certain girl, replied, "Yes and no. But a little more yes than no, if you know what I mean." Mmm, smooth. But my answer to you is the same – yes and no.

At this point you've definitely heard what I have to say on discipline and respect, so you have a philosophy now. You're miles ahead of the other dads out there, which is great. But while you were doing this, something interesting was happening. By implementing this new philosophy, you are changing. Also, thanks to both you and nature your kid is changing. The question is, What are you changing into? Let's talk about Junior first.

In this window of time your kid is starting to become a person. By that I mean he is evolving from a baby into an actual human being with a personality and opinions. But really, Who is he becoming?

Who is this kid?

Believe it or not, you have some say in this. Kids won't just become who they are going to become without being influenced by outside forces. And you, Dad, are an outside force to be reckoned with. That said, we're still being men here, right? Okay. So let's keep it real, then.

You're not special. Yeah, I said it. And lest you think I'm getting on my high horse, remember the beginning of the book. I'm not special either. So can we admit that we're not special? Pretty please? With sugar on top?

So if you're not special and I'm not special, how can our kids be? Well... It's highly unlikely. Now I'm not making fun of your kid. Or mine. And I'm not saying that your kid is not a good kid and good at many things. I'm just saying that he's not World Class.

I know, I know, "How dare you, Joe! You don't know my kid. Maybe he is World Class. Even though he comes from...y'know...our family." Well, maybe you're right; maybe I don't know. But you will. If your kid is world class at something, you will most definitely know. He'll be beating the hell out of whoever comes up against him in his specialty. It won't even be close.

Do you know when Wayne Gretzky got the nickname The Great One? When he was around ten. Ten!! They called him The Great One – as in The One For Whom We Have Been Waiting Since The Invention Of Hockey – when he was ten!! What was your nickname when you were ten? Booger?

My wife's brother (the same one from the red rod sex talk in the garage) was a phenomenal tennis player. By phenomenal I mean top-five ranked in the state of Texas from age eight to about age fourteen. Guess what he does for a living. Not tennis. He's a venture capitalist – which as I understand it has something to do with money and nothing to do with adventure. The reason he eventually quit was a kid came up behind him in the rankings. This kid went right by my brother-in-law, landed at number one, and never gave it up. My brother-in-law realized that his career might lie elsewhere because this kid was unbeatable. Care to guess who that kid was? Pete Sampras? No. Andre Agassi? Nope. It was... Richey Reneberg! Richey did go pro, but if you've heard of him you're a big tennis fan. He had some very good years and made some Grand Slam finals in doubles. I think he's a club pro now. Not bad – good, in fact - but not Hall of Fame either.

Think about it. My wife's brother, who was highly ranked for years, was not world class. The guy who overtook him and even got to go pro was, arguably, still not world class. So your kid may be world class, and if he is, congrats. But I doubt it.

Don't be down about it, though. The universe opens up to those of us who aren't great at one thing because we have time to do other things. Do you think anyone cares how good Eddie Van Halen is at volleyball? No way. We just want him to pick up a guitar. But your kid can do whatever he wants. So that's the answer. Your kid is becoming whoever he wants to be. Literally.

I realized some time ago that there is a job for everything.

If you like to build stuff, there's a job for that. If you like to knock stuff down, there's a job for that. If you like to play video games, sleep, or punch people in the face, there are jobs for those things. So don't limit your kids. Expose them to sports, art, music, phrenology (that's the reading of bumps on the head), and every other thing. Respect their decisions about what they like and who they think that they will be, and drop the expectations. Of course, if your kid gets to high school and the London Philharmonic calls, I apologize for insulting you. I was wrong.

If I'm not special, then what am I?

So we know who your kid is becoming – whoever he wants to be, with your guidance, of course. But what about you? Dads grow and evolve, right? No, wrong. You are already what you need to be. You just don't know it yet.

You are a Lion.

The Lion

You are a lion, and I mean that literally. You are a Lion with a big shaggy mane, a lioness for a wife, and lion cubs for kids. This is a biggie, and you will be quizzed on this later. So what are you? You are a Lion.

For the record, my wife hates this whole Lion thing and never wants me to talk about it. Every time I bring it up she gets this look like I'm wearing a lampshade on my head and singing songs about my genitals. But I told you going in that women won't understand this. Not only won't they understand this, if you tell them about it they won't like it. Not one bit. But guess what? Lions don't care what people think.

Start getting used to this idea: You are the daddy lion and

your family is your pride. Within a pride of lions, different lions have different roles. But the daddy lion is the most important and he sets the tone. If he's playing, everyone's playing. If he's resting, everyone's resting. And if he's mad, everyone knows it.

This idea came to me after I got to see some lions in the wild. I was watching a daddy lion just lay there while the lion cubs crawled all over him. He was all right with it and just letting the kids have some fun. But, as kids do, they started getting rougher and wilder, until the daddy lion had had enough and knocked them off his back. All the cubs got the message immediately and went to bother someone else. But one of the lion cubs came back and nipped his daddy on the ear. It was clearly a playful thing, but Daddy Lion had already spoken. That little ear nip was met with a roar and a swat that sent the cub rolling. And all around the savannah that rolling cub was the only thing moving. At the sound of the roar all the other lions froze (we people did, too).

I realized what I was seeing when I saw it. The daddy lion was the law. No question about it. And any messing with the law was dealt with immediately and harshly. When he roared, even the mama lion froze. Because they all knew what would happen if Daddy had to take this to the next level. Notice, he didn't confer with the mama lion about this. He said playtime was over, and that was that.

I can't tell you the number of times I have thought about those lions as a parent. When my kids refuse to brush their teeth or lie to me or they just won't listen, I wonder how that daddy lion would handle it. Then I do what he would do. First, I give them a gentle push in the right direction. But if I have to roar, I will. I'm perfectly okay roaring at my kids. And I mean roar, not speak to loudly. Then if they still don't get the message, like the daddy lion I take it to the next level in a hurry. That is not to say that I'm a wild animal and I hit them. I'm not and I don't. But the next level is still the next level. You'd be surprised at how removing a few luxuries from your children's lives encourages them to get back on track. No TV, no dessert, and no computer are biggies in our house. And I'm proud to say that I've never had to follow through on the threat of no after-school activities. They get the message. Daddy roared.

The trick here is to use it only when you're really mad. Lions don't filter their feelings. They don't say, "I need to show some aggression here to make my point," or "I've been roaring at little Leo a lot recently so I'll let this one slide." You need to be the same way. When you're genuinely happy, share that with your kids. But if you're mad, share that, too. Now unless you're a total hothead, you're not mad all the time. So when you are, and it's Freddy Jr.'s fault, he'll respond when you let him know. Daddy lions don't run around roaring all the time. So everyone notices when they do. You need to be the same way.

How to be a Lion

It's easy. Just let go and do what a lion would do. Other dads complain to me that their kids talk back or won't come to the dinner table or refuse to speak to them. I always think that they should be more of a Lion. Can you imagine if a baby lion refused to eat? That would be what you'd call a Starving to Death Baby Lion. The Daddy Lion doesn't care if the baby eats or not. And in the case of not listening, we already saw what happens when the baby lion doesn't do what he's told.

Some of you may think that this is harsh or even ridiculous. Maybe it is and maybe it isn't. But, it's manly, and I can tell you without a doubt that it works. Also, try to see this in a macro way as opposed to a micro way. I'm not telling you what to do in every situation every day. What I'm doing is trying to guide you toward being a more involved leader in your family and toward gaining an overall feeling of how your family should operate (according to you).

Which brings me to another valuable point about the lions. Those lion cubs will be daddy lions themselves someday (or in the case of females, mate with daddy lions). The only way they'll have to learn how to be effective daddy lions is by watching their daddy. Your kids are baby lions. They're going to learn how to be adult lions from you. If you're ineffective and indecisive and let your wife do all the work, then that's what they'll learn. But if you're strong and decisive and fun and fair, then that's how they'll be.

Do not underestimate this. This is right up there with Respect. Not only are you teaching your kids to be good people, you're teaching them to be good parents. Strong parents, with values and a point of view. You may not agree with a lion's point of view – e.g. people are food – but you have to respect that he has one, and his kids are learning it. Do yourself and your kids a favor. Be a lion.

"But, Joe, if I yell at my kids, people will see me and my kids will cry." One last time, let me reiterate. Lions don't care who hears them roar. And if your kids cry when you yell, good. They heard you loud and clear. Lion cubs don't like it when the daddy lion yells, but it doesn't hurt them. And they learn from the experience.

Chapter 7 – The Wrap-Up
   1. Discipline does not equal punishment.
   2. No bossing (again).
   3. Too many rules = Too little discipline.

4. "And then I'm going to help you do it."
5. Be creative with punishment, Sergeant Dad.
6. Your kid is not you. Let him be who he's going to be.
7. You are a Lion. Grr.

Chapter 8 – A FEW OTHER THINGS TO CONSIDER IN THIS AGE RANGE
YOUR CHILD AT 3-5 YEARS (STILL)

The emotional bank account

Since we're talking about kids acting up, I'll admit that there are times when I want my kids far far away. There are those times that I know that if my kids, a machete, and I are all in the same room together bad stuff is going to happen. This is why kids have two parents. Invariably, at least one parent will want the kids to live. Isn't it nice how that works out?

But just because kids act up doesn't make them bad people. There's a difference between character and behavior. I'm a big believer that most people have good character. They want it to be sunny, they hope their friends are healthy, they're happy to contribute to the greater good. But those same people can, on occasion, act like total assholes. Especially if they're driving. Near me. Ahem…

Anyway, your kids have this, too. They're good kids and good people who sometimes behave poorly. Just let them know that you know the difference. Just because Freddy Jr. played street baseball with your Red Sox autographed World Series ball, doesn't mean that you think that he is a bad person. You still love him; you just didn't like that behavior. You really really REALLY didn't like it. At all. So you might blow your top. Then what happens?

Think of your relationship with your kids (and your wife, for that matter) like a bank account. With your actual bank account you make sure to put money in from time to time so that when you need money you can take some out. As long as your deposits outweigh your withdrawals then you're okay. Your relationship with your kids is the same. It is an emotional bank account.

The first thing you have to do is open it by making a deposit. It can be anything. Be the coach of the baseball team. Do one of the chores that didn't get done. Tell her what a good kid she is. Then, hopefully, you make lots of deposits after that. Because the day will come when you need to make a withdrawal.

Hey, we started this whole thing by admitting that we're not perfect. So the day will come when we do something stupid in front of/to our kids. Maybe you donated his favorite lovie to charity. Maybe you forgot to pick her up from soccer. Maybe he slapped you in the face with your own belt and you called him a f*****g a*****e. On that day you'll need to have enough emotional currency to make a substantial withdrawal (which is automatic, by the way). You'll be glad that you have the currency on hand. If you're like me you've already had some real life financial challenges. Don't ruin your emotional credit with your kids. Make those deposits.

Making deposits

An easy way to make deposits is to spend time with your kids. Now this is a big-time cliché. I see all those stupid public service announcements on TV reminding us to read to our kids or tell them about drugs or to be there for them. They are always fronted by some sitcom star who just got busted for DUI and doesn't even have any kids! So let's be clear, I'm not being trite. Spending time with your kids is hard. They don't like anything cool and they're too young to do anything fun. I seriously think that if I have to play another Cranium game I'm going to go on a rampage. Also, I think that the park sucks. It is sooooo boring. When I'm watching my kids at the park I can actually feel my brain getting slower.

So the only way around it is to find stuff that you like that your kid likes, too. When my daughter was eight she became interested in music, so I got her a refurbished Ipod and I helped her download songs. Also, if there was ever a concert on TV we would watch that together. That's a good one because it ensures that she gets exposed to actual music (like Bruce Springsteen) instead of made-for-kids pop (like The Jonas Brothers).

My son loves to watch football with me (thank you, God), but he also loves to bake, which I also love. So we make muffins and cookies and cupcakes for the family. Also, we make all the birthday cakes for the whole family (except his – you can't make your own cake). He gets to run the mixer and the oven, and then he gets to eat what we make.

Since my youngest is only four, she doesn't have a lot of interests. Everyone says, "You should read to her." Bor-ing! If I want to read, I'll go to the bathroom. And I won't be reading Goodnight Moon. But I am interested in hearing my daughter talk. So I got some books that have pictures that she can point at and say, "Boat, octopus, dog, hat, bird," and it's great. She says all the words in her cute four-year-old way, and I get credit for reading to her.

Admittedly, all this takes a little creative thinking, but for my money it beats the hell out of another game of Go Fish. The bottom line is that it's okay to involve your kids in what you like to do.

Incidentally, it works for wives, too. Everyone thinks that I have the coolest wife in the world because she lets me play fantasy football, be in college football, basketball, and golf betting pools, play Xbox, and do assorted other man-friendly activities. And, yes, she's cool about it, but I'm going to take some credit here because I was smart. I involved her in everything. It was subtle at first. I asked her opinion about leagues or games, or I asked for her help on a video game, and later I asked if she wanted to join in. Currently, my wife is involved in my football pool and my basketball pool, and has her own football pool at work. It should be noted that when I say "involved" I mean that she is the defending champion in each of those leagues. So technically I'm in her leagues now. But you get the point. You can have fun together, doing things that everyone likes to do.

Core emotions

While we're on the subject of dealing with people on an emotional level, we should explore what that means. Emotions are not a topic that gets bandied about by a lot of men. I've never heard this in a bar: "Hey, Fred, did you see that the Lakers won?"
"Yeah, it was awesome."
"I know, but how did it make you FEEL?"
Aaaaaaaand Fred just lost a friend. As humans we don't think a lot about the emotions that drive us. But as men, it's downright sacrilegious. But if you're going to be dealing with kids (or a wife) – and if you're reading this book, you are – then it's time that you learned about Core Emotions.

Joe's Theory of Core Emotions goes like this: Everyone has a single core emotion that governs the way that they look at the world. In other words, out of all the emotions available to you there is one that dominates how you process information and act on it. Now this is not to say that you don't have other emotions, because you do. What it means is that one emotion is dominant, and colors, at least initially, how you process the world. The trick is to know what that core emotion is.

If asked, most people say that their core emotion is "happy". They want to be happy, they like being happy, so it must be happy. There. That was easy. Right, Joe? No, wrong. Unfortunately, if you agreed and said that your core emotion is "happy" then you are either (a) lazy, (b) ignorant, or (c) in denial. Or some combination of the three.

"But, Joe, you said you wouldn't judge me!" I'm not. I'm just saying that you're lazy, ignorant, and in denial, AND I'M OKAY WITH IT. Geez, don't be so sensitive. Anyway, the reason I say that is because I don't think that you've explored the core emotion concept enough to make a declaration of "happy" as your core emotion. Sure, you want to be happy. But is that how you look at the world?

What if you're stuck in traffic and you're going to be late for a meeting? What is your first reaction to that? Are you just happy to be alive, pursuing your goals, on this lovely day? I seriously doubt it. What if your favorite TV show goes off the air? What if someone gets in the express line at the grocery store with more than fifteen items? What if your kids need help typing a report on Sunday afternoon? What if you get a speeding ticket? What if the store doesn't have the TV that they advertised? What is your initial and consistent reaction – deep down, in your gut – to all of these things? It probably isn't "happy".

If it helps, I'll tell you what my core emotion is. It's rage. I know, surprising, right? But that's what it is. Not anger, not frustration, not upsetedness. Rage. If I'm stuck in traffic and I'm going to be late, I feel incensed that all these idiots who are in my way had the balls to all be out driving RIGHT NOW! If my favorite TV show goes off the air I can't believe what assholes everyone in America are for not liking the same show I like. If someone gets in the express line at the grocery store? Forgetabouit. I want the heads of the customer, the cashier, the store manager, and the teacher who taught this moron how to count. I mean, I've got Popsicles here!! Any number of things can set me off – the weather, TV commercials, riding the elevator only one floor, anything – and I'm off and running.

But I don't run around seeing red all the time. I have other emotions, too. And because I'm a functioning adult I realize that various situations call for a range of responses, and I force myself to react accordingly. Right about now you may be saying to yourself, "Force myself to react accordingly? I don't think so. That's phony and I'm not going to do it." Oh yeah? Ever been to a cocktail party and listened to a story that was boring you to death, but you stayed and listened anyway because you didn't want to be rude? I thought so. So shut up! See, there's my rage.

Anyway, that's what I do. And I'm perfectly okay with it. The problem with not knowing what your core emotion is is that you end up at odds with yourself – with your own hard wiring. I've had people tell me, "Joe, you can't just go around being mad all the time." But here's the interesting thing about that: Because I know that I see the world through rage – that that's who I am – I don't fight it. I don't listen to conventional wisdom that says, "You should be happy, not mad," and therefore I don't fight myself. And that makes me happy. In other words, I know that when something is truly pissing me off, that when I want to take a blowtorch to the world, I am home. I am being myself, and that makes me happy. And that helps me deal with the situation. Pretty deep, huh?

But that's why I say that your core emotion is probably not "happy". You are a much more complex person than that. And if you're honest with yourself and can reserve judgment toward which emotions are good and which ones are bad, you can discover what makes you tick. And it's awesome. Then, once you do that, you can assess the other people in your life. Like your wife.

My wife's core emotion is empathy. So she reacts

differently than I do. Stuck in traffic? Oh these poor people; I hope no one has an emergency. Favorite show goes off the air? That's too bad; all the crew is out of work. Express line? Well, I'm sure they miscounted or didn't see the sign. She literally feels for other people. As a result, she can't watch certain news stories or movies because she is too deeply affected. But on the flipside, she's the best gift giver I've ever seen. She can see into people, and every gift she gives is exactly what that person wanted – sometimes they don't even know it.

But her empathy and my rage don't always coexist well. For example, if the African kid on TV needs fifty-three cents for clean water, my wife wants to help and wonders what we can do for other kids like him. I, on the other hand, am irritated by her response. I think that the film crew filming the African kid should give him some money since they're standing right there! "And, by the way, thanks a lot for interrupting what was a fairly riveting episode of CSI, Hadji!" See the difference? But because I know who I am, and my wife knows who I am, she doesn't think that I'm evil. She just knows that that's how I see things. She just laughs and thinks that I'm joking (which I'm not, Hadji).

But let's look at you. What if you knew what your core emotion was and you were able to figure out not only what your wife's core emotion is, but what your kids' core emotions are? Ah, then we'd be on to something. Because kids have core emotions, too. It's born into them, hard-wired. And if you know what it is, then you'll know not only how you'll react to them, but how they'll react to you.

My oldest daughter has a core emotion of charity. She wants other people to be happy. Period. In fact, she cares so much about others' needs that she will forego things for herself just so other people will not be put out. She envisions their lack and tries to fill it. A few years ago when she was in first grade, her teacher, who was pregnant, yelled at the class. Kate's response was, "That's okay. She was pregnant and grumpy and probably needed to get that out." That's not how I saw it at all. In fact, her point of view sounds horrible to me, but it's important for me to understand that that's who she is so that we can communicate.

My son, on the other hand, is more negative like me. His emotion is pessimism. And at his age (8), it can very difficult for him to manage. Everything is always going to turn out wrong, and when it does it is the end of the world. Mix a little natural born rage in there and you have a volatile cocktail. It's too bad because other kids see it and invent ways to push his buttons so that he'll freak out and get into trouble. It's frustrating, but since I know that that's who he is (and it's not going to change) I'm helping him cope with it and embrace it at the same time. Just telling him to cheer up and hope for the best wouldn't work. It would only serve to frustrate him more because it diminishes his feelings and who he is.

Finally, my youngest appears to be a mix of several emotions. She definitely has rage. But I also see sorrow, defiance, and willfulness. But I think I may be honing in on her core emotion: Vengeance. I see her get angry at her brother and her sister, say that she's fine, and then later take their art off the wall and throw it away. Then, and this is the kicker, she doesn't tell them. She waits for them to see that the art is gone and then find it in the trash. She just sits back and watches it all unfold, very satisfied. Again, I'm not judging her. If my baby is a calculating, vengeful troublemaker (gulp) then so be it. That's what she and I have to deal with. But it's better to know than not to know.

In every case, discipline and respect come into play. My kids have to have the discipline to deal with who they are, both the good and the bad. My daughter's charity causes people to be attracted to her good heart (which is good). But she is totally unprepared when people take advantage of or are mean to her (which is bad). My son is always expecting that things will go wrong (bad), but he always has a Plan B and is almost never disappointed because he was ready for things to fail (good). In addition to the discipline, my kids have to respect others for who they are, since other people are invariably different from them. And I have to do all those things, too.

So what's my point? It's this: We are creatures driven by emotion, and one emotion particularly drives us more than the others. Find out what it is in you and what it is in those with whom you deal, and those dealings will go much more smoothly.

TV

Don't be afraid to use TV. I know that there is this whole segment of society that thinks that TV is evil, but I'm not part of them. Since I live in L.A. I get to hear wacky people say wacky things like, "We don't even own a TV." My response to that is, "Then what do you watch?"

I love TV. I learned to read from Sesame Street. Now with Nickelodeon and Noggin and Baby Mozart and all this cool stuff geared just for kids, I see no problem with TV. Don't let it be the only thing they do – just like you wouldn't only feed them bananas – but don't eliminate it either. And don't let people make you feel bad about it. They're your kids, and TV isn't going anywhere.

The gist of all this

So we've talked about a lot of things and you've heard a few humorous anecdotes. And all of it has a purpose. I have used everything in here in some capacity at one time or another during the course of my kids' lives. But it's new to you. And you may be thinking that it seems like a lot. Or maybe you're thinking that you want more – that it's not enough. My advice in either case is the same - Keep It Simple.

If you're overwhelmed, keep it simple because you have to. You can do this. If you're underwhelmed, try to remember that life is complicated enough, and simple is good. Simple works. But either way, with Discipline and Respect you can't go wrong.

Also, remember that this isn't something that will be going on forever. You hear about so many things that "it's a marathon, not a sprint". Well this is a sprint. The parent/child relationship changes quickly. And between the ages of about ten and twenty it changes a lot. But over the course of your child's life the bulk of the responsibility that you have for your child will be handed over to her – for better or worse. It's just the way it is. So you have to focus your efforts on building a good foundation right now because soon your kids will be building on that foundation. And they'll be doing it for the rest of their lives.

You know who else will be building on the foundation you give your kids? Their kids. So give them a good one. And while Discipline and Respect may not be the fanciest foundation for them to build on, it's sturdy. And it will last because it's something that your kids can pass on to their kids – because it's simple.

Chapter 8 – The Wrap-Up
1. The Emotional Bank Account is real. Make deposits.
2. Find out your Core Emotion first, then your wife's, then your kids'.
3. We live in an electronic age. Don't be a TV snob.
4. Keep it simple. Always.

CHAPTER 9 – LOOK AT YOU NOW
YOUR CHILD AT 5 YEARS AND BEYOND

"Get back in bed right now. Please?"

What happens when they're bigger and stronger than me?

Kids are small so that when they don't do what you want, you can physically make them do it. If they won't sit down, you sit them down. If they won't come here, you bring them here. Can you imagine what it would be like if your baby was 6'1'' and 200 pounds and didn't want a diaper change?

Once your kids are bigger and older, most of your work needs to be done because now they can physically resist you. But, hopefully, you've developed that respect and they have some discipline, so physical prowess is no longer an issue. If you haven't, then I hope you are a black belt in Tae Kwon Do and know all your pressure points. But if you are coming into this late in the game, just let me say, God love you for trying. You have put aside your ego and your pride and just said, "I can do this." And probably you can.

One thing to remember as your kids get older is that, even though it may not seem like it, you are still an actual person. You're not just "Hunter's dad". I have a friend who if you ask her a question, any question, the answer will always be phrased in the form of her kids. It's like Offspring Jeopardy.

"Okay, Janice, for $1000 what would you say the weather is like today?"

"Oh it's sunny, Vince. I had to put sunscreen on Little Timmy and Little Mary had to wear her big floppy hat to preschool. They don't like the kids to wear hats at the preschool because it's distracting, but I went ahead because she has such sensitive skin. Besides, it's not like I didn't put her name in the hat...."

So. Boring. It's like she doesn't exist except through her kids. You don't want to be that guy. You're not just Hunter's dad, you're Jeff! And Jeff likes whiskey and guns and boobs that are slightly bigger than they should be. Hunter still likes juice boxes and thinks his mom's boobs are the gold standard! Jeff knows that they're not. So feel free to be Jeff, and have your own desires, wants, and interests. At least until Hunter becomes the starting quarterback for Notre Dame. Then you'll be on TV every week and very clearly be just Hunter's dad.

Making a big deal out of small stuff

Regarding pop culture and technology, your kids are likely to come across something that you don't approve of, whatever that may be. Don't make a big deal about it. It will just make them want it more. My daughter wants to watch the TV shows Victorious and Drake & Josh. But both have a bunch of kissing and teen themes, and she's only 11. So I just told her no. I didn't freak out that she saw people kissing and groping, but I did explain to her that she's not old enough to understand that stuff (and if I have my way, won't be until age 25), and that the show is not made for eleven-year olds. Someday she can watch it, just not now. What I'm trying to avoid is the Cap'n Crunch Conundrum.

When I was growing up the only cereal I was allowed to have was Cheerios. Now Cheerios are fine, but I really wanted Cap'n Crunch. My mom flat out refused. "We're not eating sugar for breakfast!" was her reply. And that dictum lasted forever. Even when I was in high school, still no Cap'n Crunch. Well I'm 43 now. Care to guess what I eat for breakfast every day? What I just can't get enough of? Here's a hint: It ain't Cheerios. I may have missed out on eighteen years of the Cap'n, but I'm making up for it now.

I've seen this in other places, too. I knew these parents who were dead set against marshmallows. I know, marshmallows, right? What did a marshmallow ever do to them? Anyway, these parents' little girl was in my wife's kindergarten class (my wife is a teacher) and they went on a field trip to a supermarket. At the end of the trip the kids were all allowed to pick out one thing off the shelves that they could take home. Guess what the little girl picked? Yep, the biggest bag of marshmallows that they had.

It goes to the rebelling thing, which we'll talk about. But

basically, if you make something a big deal, your kids will, too. They smell the fear on you and are hard-wired to exploit it. In a way, you have them in this prison where you restrict their activities. It's for their benefit, but it's still like a prison. The trick is not to let them realize that they are in prison. Because if they don't know they're in prison, they'll never try to break out. So have your boundaries, just don't make a big deal out of them.

Answering questions

You should feel free to discuss anything with your kids. The only problem is your kids can come up with some pretty racy subjects. The trick here is to try to get out by answering in layers.

Start with the most basic, boring (but truthful) layer and keep going until they stop asking questions. It works, and it's easier than it sounds. My son asked me about his sister, "Does Kate poop out of her vagina?" So first, I didn't freak out at his use of the word vagina. I didn't make a big deal out of it, see? Then I just answered, "No." Then he asked, "Then where does she poop out of?" And I said, "Out if her dupa, like you." And he said, "Okay." That was it. He had the information that he wanted and I didn't have to get into the differences and uses of male and female genitalia. Thank God.

The same goes for more complex questions like, "Where do babies come from?" Simply, babies come from mommies. Then you can build from there. This way they can throw anything at you and you can give an honest answer without looking like they just rocked your world. What you don't want to do is what a good friend of mine did when he had to discuss sex with his eleven-year old. "Well, son, a woman is like, uh… the earth, uh, waiting for a seed… so she can grow… things. Then a, uh, farmer comes along, yeah, a farmer, and plants his seed in the earth, which has been waiting for him. Then the farmer waters the seed and lets the sun shine on the seed and the earth, and then before too long out of the ground grows... a melon! A melon grows from the farmer's seed and the earth! So that's what sex is. Understand, son?" Uh, sure, Dad.

You're a dad again

At this point you know that I have three kids. There are differences between having one or two or three kids. With one, you think, "Wow! I'm so busy! I'm a parent now! I have such a huge responsibility! Wow!" And this is true. But people with two kids look at those one-kid people like college senior looks at a first grader. "Yeah, we're both in school, but, kid, you don't even know. You'd get mauled in my world." And that is also true.

Having two kids is WAY harder than having one kid. It just is. Two baths, two dinners, two naps, two tongues to stick in the wall socket, two heads to break on the floor. The more analytical of you out there might suggest that being home alone with your one kid one-on-one is the same as having two kids at home with both parents. You would be wrong. You would be a first grader thinking that you could survive college.

Once you have three kids, you openly sneer at anyone who only has one or was so lazy as to stop at two. Two kids are suddenly quaint. They're boring and routine, and we're happy to tell you so. When you have three kids, you have to make choices because there are only two parents. If all three are crying, well one has to just keep crying. If one is hungry, one is in the bath, and one just ran out the front door, then you have to know, right then, that one kid is going hungry. In this case, the three-kid parent is like Keith Richards – just try to show him something he hasn't already seen. I will say this, though. The jump from two to three is not as hard as that from one to two.

If you have four or more kids then you are either a masochist or an 18th century aristocrat with a house full of servants. And if that's the case then I'm not even talking to you, Guvnah.

But however many kids you have, remember the rules: Respect, Discipline, No bossing. Have a reason for what you say because, gulp, they'll have all the power one day.

Rebellion

These days everyone wants to spend "quality time" and "connect" with their kids. I guess that's a good thing, but it's awfully vague. I mean, I'm not sure I connected with my parents. I definitely connected with the business end of a paddle on a few occasions. But if you're going to "connect", I do have a theory: The cooler you are, the farther your kids will have to go to rebel.

It's a known fact that all kids rebel at some point. But what they do varies, and I think it has to do with what they're rebelling against. If you're a designer-clothes wearing, nightclub-dwelling, Cristal-drinking, Ferrari-driving, man about town, then I applaud you for your take-life-by-the-balls-attitude. But your kids are going to have to do a lot for you to notice that they are rebelling. By contrast, if you're a Target-clothes wearing, study-dwelling, Diet Coke-drinking, Honda-driving, man about the house, one beer is going to make your kid feel like he's a groupie for Led Zeppelin.

Of course, I'm not saying that you have to be a dork or your kids will start a meth lab in your garage. But I am saying that if you APPEAR to be a dork, your kids won't have to go to jail to impress you. The cooler you are around them, the cooler they'll think they have to be. All you have to do is remember back to your own junior high and high school days to know that you don't want your kids to be one of the "cool" ones.

Part of this, and also very relevant, is the fact that this is not a chance for you to be cool either. You are not your kids' friend. You're older than they are, you're wiser than they are (hopefully), and you're better than they are. I mean, come on, you have a job and a house! They can't even afford to pay you rent! It's okay to have your own dorky interests. You've earned it. But in the interest of "connecting" don't reject your kids' seemingly unimportant interests outright.

Old(er) people have a way of getting set and rejecting new stuff. How many times have you heard someone say, "I can't even turn on a computer?" Or, "I wouldn't know how to operate a TiVo?" Well I'm here to tell those people that computers are here to stay and TiVo is awesome. And if you're not using either one then get on over to your neighbor Barney Rubble's house for some brontosaurus burgers.

You have to embrace new stuff. New stuff is good. People always say stupid stuff like about how it was better back in the day. Well, it wasn't. It was worse. The richest people in America one hundred years ago had a worse quality of life than you do now. They had no cars, no A/C, no TV, no Internet, no Tylenol, no plastic, and on and on and on. So deal with it, the world moves on and your kids are right in it. If they are interested in digital photography, you can learn how to use a digital camera. If they want a Nintendo 3DS, it wouldn't kill you to find out what one is. They're pretty cool. Also, knowing anything about pop culture goes a long way toward getting cred with your kids. I've heard my share of The Jonas Brothers, watched my share of iCarly, and read my share of Diary of a Wimpy Kid. Try it. It will keep you young.

Becoming your dad (an adult)

Some day soon you are going to say something and it's going to clang inside your own ears like a cowbell. You'll say to yourself, "Oh my god, that sounded just like my dad." Now this could be good news, as in, "I finally sound like my dad!" Or it could be bad news, as in, "I finally sound like my dad." There's nothing you can do about it either way because you'll feel how you feel. But it's worth mentioning because no matter how close or distant you are from your own dad, his voice got through. And the same thing will happen to your kids.

No matter what kind of screw-up or genius you are, it will not necessarily be your message that gets through. But your voice will; the little things you say and do every day. Another way of saying this is: They won't remember who you are trying to be; they will remember who you ARE. Which can be a scary thing, especially if you're not that psyched about who you are. But the bottom line is you're stuck with it – with you. And you need to buck up and embrace your fat, ugly, stupid self. Because if you can do it, your kids will see it. And someday, when they have doubts about who they are, they'll remember you and how you lived with your bad hair and creaky knees with a smile on your face, and they'll be able to do it, too.

Great things about getting older

Some people are obsessed with age. I'm about a 3 out of 10 in terms of my age obsession. It's there and I see it and I know that 50 is the next big milestone, but I also know that I could get hit by a bus tomorrow. Also, five-year olds think I'm funny, so how old could I be? But how does that help you?

It doesn't. But getting older is not so bad. And here are a

few reasons why:

- We can remember historical events because they happened during our lifetimes.
- People naturally call you "sir" instead of "son".
- The alternative is that you're dead.
- Women (for some reason) like gray hair.
- You can be fat because everyone else your age is, too.
- Cops believe what you say.
- You don't have to worry about a hair "style". If it's there at all, that's good enough.
- You're much less likely to get a speeding ticket or have the police show up at one of your parties.
- People assume that you vote.
- Your opinion (again, for some reason) matters more.
- Your body is no longer boring. It will surprise you with new pings and clicks and twitches every day.
- You don't outgrow your shoes anymore.
- People you don't like will die sooner.
- You can say "back in the day" without sounding like a tool.
- Three words: Cookies. For. Dinner.
-

Chapter 9 – The Wrap-Up
1. You are a person, not just the parent of a person.
2. Be careful what you make an issue out of.
3. All questions can be answered honestly and simply. Very simply.
4. The more kids you have, the more of a Jedi you are. And need to be.

5. Embrace your dorkness.
6. Getting old happens. Don't sweat it.

Chapter 10 – YOU'RE NOT ALONE

People say stupid things. Parents say even more. Here are a few things that you may have said or heard other parents say. Don't worry, no judgment, we all say stupid things to our kids.

- "Focus! Be serious!" (Said to a three-year old).
- "STOP SCREAMING!!"
- "Do not ever touch anyone again."
- "Pick it up off the floor and put it back on your plate."
- "Christmas is cancelled."
- "Babies come from eggs."
- "Don't spill it…(sigh)…don't step in it! (Sigh)."
- "Come here so I can spank you."
- "Beer is an adult drink. You should never drink beer."
- "OF COURSE I LOVE YOU!!"
- "Do you understand why Mommy is acting crazy?"
- "It is not okay to wipe your hands in your armpits and then smell your hands!"
- "Daddy just needs to not be near you right now."
- "It's a nice day. Why don't you go outside so Daddy can watch his show?"
- "You're making Baby Jesus cry."
- "Get your feet off the dinner table."
- "You have to eat all your food because there are starving kids in _____."

Chapter 11 – THINGS WE'VE SAID

These are a few that my wife and I have said, which I'm pretty sure are unique to us.

- "You can't have a cupcake until you finish your French fries."
- "McDonald's is closed today."
- "The beach is closed today."
- "You think I won't bite you, but I will."
- "If you hit me I'm going to punch you in the face."
- "That's a good idea. We should take a picture of your poop."
- "If you don't shut up right this second I'm going to have your mouth sewn shut."
- "You've already had a cupcake, a donut, and two Milky Way bars; so you're only having a little dessert."
- "Close your mouth when you kiss me. I'm not making out with you."
- "We can't have a dog because we have three kids. The baby is our dog."
- "YOU'RE LUCKY TO HAVE SUCH UNDERSTANDING PARENTS AS US!"
- "F**k isn't really a bad word."

Chapter 12 – WE DID DO A FEW THINGS RIGHT

These are a few things that my wife and I do with or for the kids that I think are special. They're not all original, but they all make for good parent/child interaction, and they are things that we like to do so we keep doing them.

- Go out to dinner with the kids individually.
- Make all the birthday cakes for family members.
- Give birthday presents in the morning in bed.
- Hang the kids' art instead of family photos on the walls of our house.
- Create art for gifts.
- Family movie night (but it has to be a movie that Daddy wants to watch - Ghostbusters, Karate Kid, Back to the Future, Pink Panther, etc.)
- Create a diner-style menu that the kids can order meals off of at home.
- Take driving trips instead of flying.
- Boys-only and girls-only haircuts at Mom's and Dad's respective haircut places.
- Celebrate birthday months.
- Take music lessons with the kids.

CHAPTER 13 – SO WHAT HAVE YOU LEARNED?

"Yeah about that... Do you think I could stay another year?"

Not that this is really that kind of book, but it would be nice to learn something, right? If you remember anything, remember that it's not just about love. People say, "Just love them, and that's all they'll ever need." I say, "Those people are idiots." Your kids are like your car. You put gas in it and get it cleaned, and driving it is easy. But there is a hell of a lot more going on under the hood than you are aware of on a daily basis. Your kids have a lot of moving parts, too. And you don't want to be caught surprised when they break down. So pay attention.

Know that your kids will act like you act. They're predisposed to do that. What did you expect, they even look like you! You thought that was going to be it?

With my kids, if I say or do one thing around them that they find remotely interesting, they copy it for months - especially if it's a cuss word. Sometimes it's fun. At one point I had our baby cabbage patching, raising the roof, and, my favorite, fake laughing. It was like cocktail party laughing. Like when you're with other adults and someone tells some story that they think is hilarious, but you don't, so you go, "Ah ha ha ha," and then pray that you get struck by lightning before you die of boredom. My daughter had that laugh down cold. She even used it when I wasn't being as funny as she would have liked.

In other instances, it's not so fun. When she was nine, my other daughter perfected her look of disbelief followed by saying, "What the hell??" She wouldn't stop, and my wife was positive that she was going to have to go pick her up at the principal's office. But I don't get worked up about stuff like that. Life is too short. Which is not to say that language might not be a priority for you. It may, and you may be more relaxed about something else. That's fine because you're an adult and you can think for yourself. Teach your kids to do the same.

Your kids are going to be adults themselves someday, and they're going to have a strong desire to think about and react to things the same way you do. But they're not you. They can be Democrats. Or Republicans. Or Christians or Jews or Atheists. I know, it's radical. What can I say, I'm a nut. But someday your kids are going to be forty. Do you really want them looking to others about how to think? Really?

Remember, thou art mortal. You're as full of it as the next guy and you're going to screw up. Your kids should know that. But they should also know that even though you screw up you're always trying to be the right person. And they'll try, too.

So there. That wasn't so painful, right? We laughed a little, we got a few good ideas, and we kept the words big and the pages thick. Look, you're a good person. You read the book, right? And you want your kids to be good people, too. You can be confident that they will be if for no other reason than the world doesn't ask that much of most of us. I don't know about you, but I haven't had the nuclear launch codes lately.

Now, after reading this you may be thinking, "What the hell, Joe? I just spent my whole weekend reading this book and I still think you're full of shit." Guess what? You're right, and I applaud you. You're thinking for yourself rather than just trusting me because I wrote a book. Good! And I never said I was more qualified than you. I only said that I've had remarkable success. Now that you know what I know, it should go even better for you.

As you start to look at things differently, you'll see yourself changing. Not a lot, a little. You'll become more confident, more in charge, more in tune. When that happens, let it. You're becoming a lion. Be a lion and your kids will be lions, too.

Good luck, Dad. See you on the savannah.

ADDENDUM 1 – KEY PHRASES TO REMEMBER

- Discipline and Respect.
- I don't do that to you, so please don't do that to me.
- Either you do it or I'm going to help you do it.

There, how hard is that?

ADDENDUM 2 – YOUR FINAL TOOLBOX

- Don't worry; you are learning at the same pace as the baby.
- Feed me, change me, burp me, sleep me.
- Get a sleep book and read it.
- React the way you want your kid to react.
- Give respect to get respect.
- Keep it simple.
- You are not special.
- You are a Lion.
- Discipline and punishment are different things.
- Discipline removes the need for rules.
- Be firm, but be fun and creative.
- Open an Emotional Bank Account.
- Discover your Core Emotion.
- Appear to be a nerd.
- Remember, if I can do this, you can do it, too.

CONTACT ME

It's not easy to get everything you need from a book – especially a short book. Sometimes your problem is too specific. Or sometimes it helps just to have someone explain it to you. If that's the case, contact me.

One of the advantages of publishing this book independently is that there is no one to get between you and me. No publisher, no marketing people, no public relations people – just you and me. And I like that. I feel that books like this (and maybe books in general) should be more interactive. When I finish reading a book, if I want to keep poking around in that world for a while, I should be able to. Well, here you can.

I meant what I said at the beginning of the book. I believe in this stuff and I think you can do it. So email me with any questions, stories, comments, concerns, additions, or whatever. I'll get back to you and we'll figure it out. Heck, if you have a good suggestion, I'll add it to the book. Not bad, right? Imagine if you could do that with other authors. "Hey JK Rowling! You can't do that to Dumbledore!" JK Rowling wouldn't respond. But I will, I promise. If you actually read this whole book it is the least I can do.

Leave a comment at www.theirreverentdad.com
The Irreverent Dad on Facebook
@IrreverentDad on Twitter
or email: TheIrreverentDad@earthlink.net

Joe Reilly
May 13, 2011

ABOUT THE AUTHOR

Joe Reilly is a screenwriter and father of three living in Los Angeles. Other jobs Joe has held include baker, lifeguard, carpenter, waiter, data analyst, swim teacher, lacrosse coach, and management consultant. Most recently, Joe wrote, produced, directed, and starred in a movie entitled Effin Sports Camp, which has been optioned by Paramount Pictures.

But none of that matters...

...to anyone other than publishers, who want something to put on the backs of books. What matters is that Joe is a regular guy who somehow has become an excellent dad. Joe likes sports, food, video games, beer, movies, and the bikini issues of most magazines. He has all the regular guy problems: kids, a wife, bills, no money, too small of an apartment, and not enough time. He especially doesn't have time to read books on the side about how to do stuff he's already doing. But by applying a few fundamental techniques he has found a way to consistently be a better dad than he had any reason to believe he could be.

Made in the USA
Lexington, KY
29 December 2012